SHOWMAN

The Life and Music of
Perry George Lowery

CLIFFORD EDWARD WATKINS

University Press of Mississippi / *Jackson*

www.upress.state.ms.us
The University Press of Mississippi is a member of the
Association of American University Presses.

Copyright © 2003 by University Press of Mississippi
All rights reserved
Manufactured in the United States of America

11 10 09 08 07 06 05 04 03 4 3 2 1

Library of Congress Cataloging-in-Publication Data

Watkins, Cifford E.
Showman : the life and music of Perry George Lowery / by
Clifford Edward Watkins.
p. cm.—(American made music series)
Includes bibliographical references (p.) and index.
ISBN 1-57806-555-0 (cloth : alk. paper)—
ISBN 1-57806-556-9 (pbk. : alk. paper)
1. Lowery, P. G. (Perry George), 1870–1942. 2. Cornet
players—United States—Biography. 3. Afro-American
musicians—Biography. I. Title. II. Series.
ML419.L69W382 2003
788.9'6'092—dc21   2003002405

British Library Cataloging-in-Publication Data available

Good Things Cometh to
He Who Waiteth so Long as
He Hustleth while He Waiteth

—P. G. LOWERY

CONTENTS

FOREWORD

Clifford Edward Watkins's biography of Perry George Lowery offers a unique life and time of an American musician and bandleader. Lowery's career spanned more than half a century, from the 1880s into World War II. Billed as the "World's Greatest Colored Cornet Soloist" and called the angel "Gabriel's right-hand man" by W. C. Handy, an admiring rival and the author of "St. Louis Blues," Lowery was a band and orchestra leader, showman, manager, and entrepreneur who toured the North, Midwest, West, and border states. He had his own companies, headed minstrel shows, and led circus bands, headlining the Ringling Brothers–Barnum and Bailey sideshows from 1919 to 1931. As a touring artist, his career began with railroad travel and, except for the last two years, ended with convoys of trucks in "motor shows."

Born in Topeka, Kansas, in 1869, Lowery grew up in a rural Kansas Flint Hills community. His family homestead had been founded as part of a black western migration. He came from a musical family and found inspiration in rural Kansas throughout his life. Eureka, Kansas, followed his career and celebrated his accomplishments long after his death. Though he studied at the Boston Conservatory of Music, he earned the honorific title *professor* through his musical talents, not academic training; the term reflected how much his students and peers respected him. After playing with the Nashville Students Company, Lowery came to head that company as well as minstrel shows. He headlined circus sideshows as a bandleader, though African-Americans could not play under the big top. Lowery performed first with his family's brass band and then with local and regional colored bands. At the turn of the century, he began to head minstrel shows and bands, performing in small-town opera houses across America as well as New York City's Madison Square Garden. His friend Scott Joplin often wrote and arranged music for Lowery's group. Lowery also managed bands, shows, and P. G. Lowery's Progressive Musical Enterprise, which ran as many as three touring companies at the same time. Lowery became a mainstay of the traveling music circuit. As a musician, he began at a time when every local community had its own bands—black and white—but by the time of his death in 1942, recorded music and radio had diminished the American band traditions.

Watkins's study of Lowery is carefully and thoroughly researched. On Lowery's trail for more than twenty years, Watkins has reconstructed much of the bandleader's touring career from reports Lowery sent to the *Indianapolis Freeman* and the *Eureka (Kansas) Herald*. In the late nineteenth and early twentieth centuries, the *Freeman* was the staple of the segregated African-American entertainment industry. With its "The Stage" columns, the *Freeman* was, in Watkins's words, the "circulatory system of black show business." Watkins has discovered many reviews and reminiscences about Lowery as well as surviving letters and documents. In the process, Watkins has recovered an important but too often neglected part of the American past: African-American contributions to performance band traditions. He reconstructs a time when nearly every town had an African-American band, while well-known regional and national bands and shows crisscrossed the United States (and Canada and sometimes Europe), entertaining black and white audiences.

An innovator, a musician at the top of his craft, and a successful businessman, Lowery still struggled in a United States in which African-Americans faced racial discrimination on a daily basis. He helped to promote vaudeville and to move black entertainment away from the stereotyped minstrel show, but he could not escape it completely. He tried to abandon old minstrel routines, introducing ragtime and cakewalk dancing. At various times in 1904 and 1906, for example, Lowery billed his company as "Not a Minstrel Show," but he found that he had to return to a minstrel format in circus sideshows. Though a headliner in the sideshows for America's most prestigious circuses, he remained barred from performing under the big top, which was reserved for white bands and performers. When he traveled, he had his own private *Pullman* car, and at one time his company traveled in three such private railroad cars. While offering luxurious surroundings, these accommodations also served to insulate Lowery and his touring company from the humiliations and second-class status of a Jim Crow United States that often barred African-Americans, regardless of their status, from staying and eating in center city hotels and restaurants. A private railroad car was both a luxury and a necessity.

Watkins draws on personal insights from his long career as a musician, touring artist, bandleader, teacher, and scholar. He understands and explains the world of African-American musicians and their roles in the black and white communities and American culture. It was a world of both hard knocks and—for some—ease, of both insecurity and potential fame, and of both silence and applause. In the process, African-Americans were creating new forms of popular culture. Watkins reminds us that live music was central to much of American entertainment, especially travel-ing minstrel shows, circuses, carnivals, and vaudeville. For the touring musician, Watkins tells us, going on the road "could prove to be a hard teacher and a demanding taskmaster." It was a culture of "shammers" and "jammers"—fakers and real players.

Watkins relates an earlier time when black artists were ubiquitous in a mostly segregated entertainment business. It was an age before black per-formers in post–World War II America became a major presence in com-mercial entertainment—in popular music, jazz, the blues, sports, stand-up comedy, and television.

I first met Cliff Watkins in 1996, when he was bringing to a close his research on and biography of Lowery. Cheryl Lester and I codirected a

National Endowment for the Humanities summer seminar on African-American migration and communities held at the University of Kansas in Lawrence. As a seminar participant, Cliff brought Lowery and black band traditions alive for us. At the same time, he embraced Lawrence's black community by playing at services at local black churches. The spirit, gregariousness, commitment, musicality, and scholarship that Watkins brought to Lawrence in the summer of 1996 infuses his work on Lowery.

DAVID M. KATZMAN
Professor of American Studies
University of Kansas

ACKNOWLEDGMENTS

This project represents the total of a tremendous amount of support from a number of very wonderful people. P. G. Lowery was a masterful entertainer and skillful organizer. His music gave pleasure to many people.

I first acknowledge Reginald Thomasson of Orangeburg, South Carolina; Pat Foster, a Kansan living in Tallahassee, Florida; and Frank T. Greer of Nashville, Tennessee. While I was investigating African-American college and university band directors some years ago, these people spoke in glowing and reverential terms about a black circus bandleader named P. G. Lowery. I promised myself that when I finished my current project, I would investigate this seemingly remarkable man.

In 1982, Professor Eileen J. Southern accepted me into her National Endowment for the Humanities summer seminar for college teachers held at Harvard University. After reviewing my project plan, she provided the tools for the Lowery research.

The Yale University microfilm department offered additional resources. I greatly appreciate the cordiality and assistance of noted anthropologist John Szwed.

The Parkinson Research Center at the Circus World Museum in Baraboo, Wisconsin, rests on the site that was the winter quarters of the

Ringing Brothers Circus and the home of the Ringling family. The intellectual ringmaster, Fred Dahlinger, presiding over this now amazing repository of circus documents, provided many rare items that supported the project.

In Philadelphia I met the unique Robert Houston, the proprietor of the Philadelphia Mini Circus and Museum (also known as the Philadelphia Museum of the Circus), who claims to be the only African-American who owns both a Tangley air calliope and a working steam calliope. Rob also is the collector/owner of an astounding assemblage of circus memorabilia, including photographs of P. G. Lowery.

An old friend and circus aficionado from my school days in Knoxville, Tennessee, Paul "P. T." Richards became a great supporter. P. T., who has an uncanny way of discovering obscure tidbits of show information, managed to push me forward intellectually, especially on the project's down days. He has also built a collection of O-gauge railroad memorabilia, circus wagons, and other collectibles called Richards's Great Circus. Paul's talent helped in the development of this project and a spin-off, the revival of the P. G. Lowery Star of the West Brass Band. Thanks again, Paul, and Geoff Stelling and Wayne Clark. Eureka—we pulled it off!

In Boston, William A. Seymour, president of the Boston Conservatory, became interested in his famous alumnus and pledged the resources of his institution in finding any further evidence of the presence of Lowery and of his teacher, H. C. Brown.

I recognize Dr. David Katzman and Dr. Cheryl Lester, professors of American studies at the University of Kansas at Lawrence, for their assistance in locating data on the Great Migration.

People in Lowery's home area of Eureka, Kansas, provided first a little information via Nancy Beitz, who managed the Greenwood County Historical Society, and then more from Helen Bradford, a prolific writer for the society. Bob Hodge, who indexes newspapers in the area, seemingly knows the location of everything written. These people, plus Deke and Zenith Lindamood, Edward and Normalie Bobbitt, and many other citizens, made my initial visit to Eureka one of the most unforgettable experiences of my life. There simply are not enough good words to describe their hospitality.

Recognition is also in order for other residents of the area who shared information with me. Hap Jackson, a cowboy who rode with P. G. Lowery's nephew, Gene, told me stories about their adventures. Hap has traded his horse for a wheelchair, but he still rides tall in the saddle.

Other supporters included my uncle, J. B. Wheeler of Knoxville, Tennessee, a friend of Lowery's, and Mrs. George McDade, widow of Little George McDade, the Boy Wonder of Knoxville Tennessee. Uncle convinced Mrs. McDade to share a few pages of the diary that George kept as he traveled with the shows. I must also acknowledge Roz Franklin, the "Cleveland Connection"; my wife, Sally, who has endured this whole process; and my kids—Becky, Chip, and grandson Jacob—who have all wondered if Dad would ever finish this project.

There are some other folks whose names I may have forgotten or perhaps, apologetically, I never knew. They unobtrusively (in the style of Lowery) came onto the scene, provided their help, and quietly moved on. I am grateful to all of you.

Praise God, from whom all blessings flow.

PROLOGUE

I sat in a compartment on Amtrak's *California Zephyr* as it passed through Colorado's stunningly beautiful Glenwood Springs Canyon on a clear sunny November day in 1993. I wondered how often P. G. Lowery must have passed over these same rails in his *palace* car, *Pana*, coupled onto a circus train almost a century earlier. How many times did he see this same breathtaking scenery, or did he visualize something different on each trip? His business associates readily acknowledged that Lowery had an entrepreneur's vision and that he was an unusual sight to see. People who couldn't afford a ticket would often go to the railroad yards to see a black man who owned a ten-thousand-dollar railroad car. Actually, he owned several of them. Lowery also owned and operated a very successful business enterprise. His vision provided the best of entertainment for millions, and he offered employment for hundreds of people during his prime. His engaging personality and amazing musical talent had an uncanny way of drawing people together. Although he has been deceased for more than a half century, interest in Lowery's talent and personality still draws people together.

On a clear, sunny, Sunday morning, I walked down the middle of the main street of Eureka, Kansas, starting from the railroad siding near where the Missouri Pacific station stood, past the old bank building and the stately three-story Greenwood Hotel. By the time I passed the Eureka Bank building and the *Herald* offices, my gait had become less that of a leisurely stroll and more of a precise stride. As I passed the old bandstand and courthouse sites, the Eureka Opera House, which is now apartments and Bill's Grocery Store, came into view. Other passers-by could probably hear my unabashed humming of "Barnum and Bailey's Favorite." My footsteps matched the cadence of an unseen but strongly felt show band.

Lowery traversed this same route many times. Unloading from that railroad siding, he paraded his show into the opera house as his music reverberated off those stately old buildings. The windows of those structures undoubtedly held many townsfolk watching his triumphal returns home. Whether with the circus or the Nashville Students Company or for a solo appearance, the return of the man that Eureka claimed as its son brought about spontaneous acclaim. His music did not die. The notes generated by the Lowery family's Star of the West Brass Band still ring. The rhythmic sounds of the cadential footfalls spawned by those early marching bands remain permanently embedded in the environment. If one is really quiet, echoes of those bands—loud and clear, high and mighty—can be heard.

The Lowery farm was located just outside of Reece, Kansas, alongside an area called Duke Hill. A roadway was built through the site of the family cemetery. The excavation desecrated the little cemetery plot, leaving a few misaligned footstones. Overseeing this scenario is a veteran's headstone, inscribed, "Thomas Cracraft, Tate Co. C, 121 U.S. Colored Troops, Died Jul 1, 1892, Aged 76 Yrs." Someone has placed an American flag and some flowers on the grave. Although the little flag is tattered and the plastic wreath of flowers is in disarray, we know that someone made an effort to remember. The band inside of me became muffled, playing a funeral dirge for the original seven industrious families that came here after the Civil War in search of the American dream: the Wrights, the Greggs, the Dukes, the Wilsons, the Lowerys, the Greenes, and the Washingtons. After overcoming overwhelming odds in life, did they all fall prey, in their final resting places on Duke Hill, to a Kansas roadway?

These seven families appreciated their lot in life and gave their best to Greenwood County, to Kansas, and to the world. From these families came Bishop John Gregg, the first person of African descent selected for the presidency of Howard University in Washington, D.C. Perry George Lowery, the World's Greatest Colored Cornet Soloist, joined Gregg in receiving international acclaim and recognition. Now the band is playing again in a lively fashion

This book seeks to recognize and continue the sprit of Perry George Lowery, the man who lived and exemplified the philosophy that "Good things cometh to he who waiteth, so long as he hustleth while he waiteth."

CLIFFORD EDWARD WATKINS I

SHOWMAN

THE FLINT HILLS SETTLERS

The vision of an agrarian West certainly appealed to many people, like the Lowerys, who sought to improve their lot in life. Benjamin "Pap" Singleton, who openly claimed to be "the whole cause of the Kansas Migration," began organizing movements from Tennessee and perhaps from bordering states into Kansas around 1870. According to Nell Irvin Painter, Singleton "took enormous interest in the welfare of the race, and . . . grew convinced that blacks could prosper only outside the old slave states".[1]

Singleton's projects subscribed to the premise that Kansas was the place where black people could live with peaceful dignity and respect in a truly free society. In 1869 Singleton and Columbus M. Johnson made an exploratory trip into Kansas. Johnson remained in Topeka as the advance agent for Singleton's Edgefield Real Estate Association. Singleton then returned to Nashville, Tennessee, and began organizing excursions into Kansas. "While blacks in the Deep South set their sights on Liberia, a steady stream of migrants flowed from three Border States to Kansas. Instead of entertaining thoughts of Liberia, blacks [from] Kentucky, Missouri and Tennessee established small colonies on the western prairies or in Kansas cities and towns. The movement was gradual, and little is known of its progress, particularly from the neighboring state of Missouri." Although around 1879 this "Exoduster" movement brought many people of color from the South into Kansas during the Great Migration, other African-Americans had previously relocated there. William Loren Katz stated that "Of course not all black migrants came west as part of the exodus. Some had arrived soon after the emancipation, part of the huge wagon trains that rolled and bumped across the prairies after the Civil War. Some black westerners had arrived during the war, escaping a life of bondage."[2]

HOMESTEADING ON SPRING CREEK

The flint hills of Kansas are located in "the central third of the eastern half of the state." After the Civil War, the region was attractive to the cattle industry, which shipped animals to be fattened on the abundant bluestem grass. In 1905 the *Emporia Gazette* reported that a circle with a radius of fifty miles around the town of Emporia would include eight of the greatest cattle counties in Kansas. Adjacent to that land was rich soil that farmers greatly desired. "Many of the first settlers to reach the Flint Hills . . . passed through the region's tall grass, preferring the rich, deep-soiled plow lands further west. Only a few stopped to take up land in the fertile valleys along the several streams that permeate the region."[3]

During the nineteenth century, Greenwood County, Kansas, attracted settlers from many cultures, most prominently French families who moved into the northern part of the county. Swiss and German farmers inhabited the Lamont area, and Norwegians established the Fall River–area communities of Lapland and Christiana. People of African descent settled in the Spring Creek area of the county, south of Reece.

African-Americans appear first to have settled in Greenwood County at some point during the 1860s. Particularly in the county's western areas, Greenwood strongly opposed slavery, and residents welcomed black settlers as neighbors. The *Herald* indicated that Alex Gregg Jr., a teamster, arrived in Greenwood County around 1870. Gregg probably was one of Greenwood County's first African-American residents. Other black families joined the Greggs—the Wrights, Dukes, Wilsons, Lowerys, Washingtons, and Greens. These families filed claims on their land and set about working in various venues. The women worked as household servants, and the men worked as farm hands for neighbors, cleaned the courthouse and its grounds, dug graves and helped to build the new roads, and hunted wolves for the bounty they carried.[4]

An ever-growing number of black citizens joined the burgeoning Spring Creek community. The 1870 census included William and Lavinia Slupter and their seven children as well as Andrew and Rachel Lowery and their seven children. By 1875, three more families had come to the area, including Payton and Mary Polley and their eight children; Henry and Selah Banks and their seven children; and F. P. Smith, his wife, and two children. Banks gained a degree of notoriety in 1875 by raising an ear of corn that was thirteen and a half inches long. The *Herald* reported in 1870 that the Perry Washingtons were finishing a new house and that Washington and Alex Gregg had been paid four dollars for cleaning the courthouse well in October 1875.[5]

The 1880 census rolls recorded three additional families of African descent: John W. Wright, age seventy-five, and his three sons; Mark and Charity Wright and their eight children; and Thomas Cracraft, a Civil War Veteran, and his wife. The 1885 record included John W. Wright Jr. and his wife, June, and their two children, and the 1895 record included the families of Charles J. and Georgia Jones, Bart and Jane McCullough, and I. N. "Nye" Duke and Rose Duke.[6]

As the black residents established themselves, their civic involvement heightened. Perry Washington attended the 1872 Republican county convention and was influential in the nomination of candidates for county offices. He also was involved in the temperance movement and in 1873 met with one such group to nominate anti-liquor-license, antisaloon candidates for mayor and county council. Seymour Lowery also participated in this movement.

Some of the census reports indicated that many black heads of households were unable to read or write. To ensure that their children would be educated, these families readily enrolled their youngsters in the Miles School, located in Reece, where they apparently met with success. In 1877, Johnny Polley was listed on the honor roll, and Perry Lowery, Edward Green, and Eugene Lowery were cited for averaging 93 percent or better. In 1882, Frankie Polley made the honor roll. Not to be outdone, many adults enrolled in a type of adult education program in which they learned to read the local newspaper and the Bible.[7]

Grace Dobler indicated that during this developmental period, "members of the Second Congregational Church (black) built a parsonage at 4th and Oak Streets. They held services in the courthouse until they built their church."[8]

Summarizing the development of Greenwood County's black community, Zenith Lindamood stated, "In the fifty years since the end of the Civil War, sixteen black families had settled in western Greenwood County, some of them being the married children of the first black settlers. In other cases the settlers had moved on to other places. Those who remained organized a Sunday School, participated in temperance meetings, petitioned to get roads opened, and served as township officers. Several of them managed to prove out on their claims and received title to them."[9]

Relations among different cultures and especially between black families and others ran the gamut from cooperation and respect to intolerance. According to a history of Greenwood County, "Much of the history of the treatment of black people in Greenwood County is not a pretty story. Although initially an avid anti-slavery county, in the early years of [the twentieth] century and especially in the 1920s, the egalitarian ideals of the early settlers were replaced by virulent racism. White intolerance of blacks developed and was promoted by active racist organizations." Other reports indicate that overt acts of racism may have been aberrations, failing to accurately reflect the attitudes of the entire citizenry. The authors of the county history had no doubt that these families earned the community's respect through their collective hard work, participation, and enterprising spirit: around the turn of the century, whites described their black neighbors as "hard-working, thrifty and good citizens."[10]

FAMILY #158

The Homestead Act of 1862 and the 1873 Timber Culture Act offered qualifying homesteaders free land in a large part of the developing West. Many black settlers traveled well into western Kansas's prairie, often planning to stake out their claims in Graham County, the site of Nicodemus, an all-black settlement.[11]

For reasons that remain unknown, however, Andrew Lowery and his family settled more to the east, on a remote farm in the Spring Creek area. The Lowerys claimed this acreage just after the Civil War In a land rush There is no evidence to indicate that they were a part of any large migration. As reasonably successful farmers, they maintained a high degree of self-sufficiency. Greenwood County Courthouse records show that on March 10, 1880, Lowery received a patent of landownership from the federal government, having met all of the residency and progress provisions—what was known as proving out his claim.[12]

The 1875 Census identified the Lowerys only as "Family #158." The census did not report that the Lowerys were entertainers who were open and friendly to all those they met. Their hospitality was legendary among both blacks and whites. The Lowerys would not hesitate to host large numbers of people or a single stranger, serving fresh cider from their apple orchard, ice cream, cake, and lemonade. Each Lowery played a musical instrument, and all family members were capable singers. Before the family members went their separate ways as a result of marriages and various individual pursuits, they organized a brass band that played at community social events, in the church at Reece, and in Eureka. The band members were esteemed for their willingness to perform whenever invited to do so. Their band apparently was strong enough to gain some notoriety, and in March 1875 the *Herald* printed a challenge issued over Seymour Lowery's name as bandleader: "The Star of the West Brass Band of Eureka hereby challenge[s] the Eureka Brass Band to a trial of skill, at any time within sixty days, for a sum of money not to exceed $50.00 a side, or for the supper, as they may prefer."[13]

Brass bands were quite the rage by the end of the Civil War, and the Lowery family band apparently met with great success in the Eureka area. However, instruments often were put aside for more important pursuits. During the first years after their arrival in Kansas, proving out their claim must have been their primary goal: failure to meet the requirements would result in forfeiture of the land.

Their work was well rewarded. The 1875 Kansas census described the Lowery holdings as ninety acres of fenced land and seventy acres not fenced. There were two hundred rods of stone fencing and four hundred rods of wire fencing. The family's inventory included one hundred dollars worth of farm tools and machinery. The Lowerys had fifty dollars worth of poultry, three horses, thirty-one head of cattle, and two dogs. The farm also contained 125 apple trees, with 75 of them bearing fruit; 18 pear trees, with 6 not bearing fruit; 310 peach trees, only 10 not bearing fruit; 4 bearing plum trees; and 70 cherry trees, with 10 not bearing fruit. Produce that year included sixty acres of corn, two acres of Irish potatoes, ten acres of millet and grain, and eighty acres of prairie hay. The Lowerys marketed one hundred dollars worth of garden produce, slaughtered or sold for slaughter one hundred dollars worth of animals, and made four hundred pounds of butter.[14] Oil deposits subsequently were discovered on the land. Although as a result of certain socially predetermined expectations, some neighbors regarded the Lowerys' agricultural achievements as unusual, most other residents admired the family; the rest tolerated them.

After the Lowery family had proved out its claim, its members once again took up their band instruments. Since the Spring Creek residents were politically involved, certain events called for the band's presence. Dobler reported that "in October 1880, two loaded passenger coaches left Eureka for a Republican rally held in the new town of Gould City (now called Severy). Among the passengers was the Eureka black band (referred to as 'colored' in that era) and the Drum and Fife Band of Eureka. The colored ladies of Eureka gave a supper at the courthouse for the purpose of raising funds to buy new uniforms for the colored brass band."[15]

Andrew Lowery and Rachel Tucker Lowery came to Kansas from Virginia or possibly what is now West Virginia. Andrew was born in Marion, Ohio, and he and Rachel married in 1847. They subsequently moved to Ohio, where their children James, Seymour, Matthew, Edward, Mary, Jesse, and Anetta (Nettie) were born. In 1869 the family traveled to Kansas, where Perry George was born, finally settling in Reece in 1870.[16]

Rachel Lowery died on November 26, 1880. Andrew later remarried, taking for his bride the former Mary E. Green, a widow, although the exact date of this marriage is unknown. Andrew's obituary says he married Mary in 1892; however, a story in the *Herald* dated March 9, 1882 reported that "Mr. Andrew Lowery of Spring Creek returned after an absence of some months . . . induced a particular lady friend of his to consent to come back with him and accompany him through the balance of his life's journey." Andrew and Mary may have known each other before their prior marriages. She was the mother of two children, Ulysses and Edward Green. Ed, a trombonist, would become Perry Lowery's close friend and mentor and would be instrumental in starting P. G. in show business.[17]

Andrew Lowery died on September 28, 1899, at the age of seventy-nine. He had been an active member of the Greenwood County community, serving on the governing board of the Sabbath School Association and leading a petition to establish an important road. His widow, Mary, was living alone in 1905 and died in 1933 at age eighty-nine. Local lore holds that she is buried in the Reece Cemetery, which generally was reserved for whites, although some exceptions apparently were made.[18]

Rachel and Andrew's oldest child, James, born in 1851 in Ohio, owned properties in Oklahoma. He was an attorney who developed a successful business as a real estate agent and land speculator. On April 29, 1886, James married Olive Cannon in Reece.[19]

James later became business partners with his youngest brother, Perry. In December 1811, James arrived in Indianapolis with a railroad car valued at two thousand dollars, which he presented to his brother as a gift. "Uncle Jim," as he was known, died in April 1912.[20]

Andrew and Rachel Lowery's second son, Seymour, born in 1853 in Ohio, served as the director of the family brass band. Seymour filed a land claim in 1884, and the 1885 Kansas census lists him as widowed and living with his son, William Eugene Lowery. Little else is known about Seymour, but Gene earned great recognition as a cowboy.[21]

Gene attended the Miles School from 1887, when he was eight, until 1897. Gene played tuba in the Lowery family band. Helen Bradford described him as a pasture manager in the Flint Hills grasslands, a position in which he supervised herds of cattle sent from Texas for fattening on their way to eastern packinghouses. By his death in 1923, Gene had become a highly respected cowboy, foreman, and brand reader for the Texas cattle shipping syndicates, known throughout the Texas panhandle, Oklahoma, and New Mexico. The *Eureka Democratic Messenger*, which printed an editorial when he died, stated, "when you take notice that 'Gene' Lowery was a . . . black man, you begin to sit up and take notice and wonder after all if the color line that has for years stood as a barrier, may not at times become obliterated and forgotten as it certainly has in the case at hand, for 'Gene' Lowery stood aces high with everybody, and everybody was his friend. . . . The Cattlemen agree that they will probably never find another man just like Eugene Lowery, Black or white."[22]

Eugene Lowery's cattleman friends demonstrated their esteem for him by insisting that he be buried in the white Reece Cemetery, where they had purchased a plot and a headstone for him. The *Herald* ran a notice thanking friends who had helped the family during its bereavement, signed by his widow, Maude, and by Mrs. R. J. Mack, and Mr. George Lowery, probably Gene's children.

Matthew, Andrew and Rachel's third child, was born in 1855 and was "insane," a term that at that time had various meanings, including mental deficiencies and physical limitations or deformities. His disappearance from subsequent records gives credence to the possibility that Matthew was institutionalized outside of Greenwood County. An 1888 newspaper item reported that a "son of Andrew Lowery died (a young man), severe attack of bilious colic."[23] This may have been a reference to Matthew.

On the fourth child, Edward, very little has been discovered except in the censuses of 1870, 1875, and 1880, which list his ages as thirteen, nineteen, and twenty-four, respectively. He died on March 19, 1882, of pneumonia at his father's residence. Of Mary, Andrew and Rachel's oldest daughter and fifth child, all that is known is her ages according to various censuses: eleven in 1870, seventeen in 1875, and twenty-two in 1880.[24]

Andrew and Rachel's sixth child was Jesse Lowery. He filed for final proof on his claim to 160 acres of land in the Otter Creek Township, Kansas, in August 1884, right around his twenty-first birthday. He later became an attorney, residing in the Indian Territories in the city of Okmulgee. Jesse reportedly was one of the first purchasers of land in Oklahoma. He died in December 1921 and was buried in Reece.[25]

Anetta (known as Nettie and sometimes cited as Nellie), the seventh child and second daughter of Andrew and Rachel, married Peter Wright in Greenwood County on May 5, 1887. Ten years later, the sad news circulated that "Peter Wright (Lowery son-in-law) died, leaving a widow and several small children in limited financial circumstances." He was buried in the Lowery cemetery. When Perry Lowery died in 1942, Nettie was his only surviving sibling.[26]

Perry George Lowery, Andrew and Rachel's eighth child, was born in 1869. Little information is available concerning Perry's academic work. Records show only that he attended the Miles School from 1888, when he was eighteen, until 1889. He would make his mark as a musician. Perry, the youngest member of the Lowery family's band, started out as the drummer. In 1931, Edwin Walters reminisced in the *Eureka Herald* about his early life in Greenwood County, remembering "a little colored boy who when five years old came as a snare drummer in a colored fife and drum corps . . . to play at a fourth of July celebration held at Branson's Grove. . . . This little drummer boy was dressed in a blue jacket, red short trousers, white stockings that reached above his knees. I heard him play at Siloam springs, Arkansas, in April of 1895, when he was twenty-five. I have often wondered if he is living now." The *Herald*'s editor added, "the drummer boy is Perry Lowery, now leader of Lowery's Band and Minstrel with the Ringling Bros. Circus. His mother, Mrs. M. E. [Green] Lowery, lives near Reece."[27]

According to Lowery, he came to take up the cornet only after the family's band failed:

My brothers took up other vocations in life, and I was forced to leave school very young to work on the farm.

I found an old cornet in the attic and began to practice on it, to prove music was a profession. After my brothers efforts was a failure my parents strongly opposed my trying to make music a success. They would not let me have my old cornet in the house; so I practiced in the barn. I continued for several years until I became a very good cornetist. After experience in a local band I took it up as a profession.

Any doubts about his musical ability were dispelled, however, when in June 1895, he enrolled in the Boston Conservatory of Music. Lowery received concentrated training, which would have included musical composition and theory in addition to studio instruction on his instrument.[28]

Having left the family farm, Perry would now start to contribute to Family #158 in other, unique ways.

GOING ON THE ROAD

From the beginning, the nature of P. G. Lowery's career demanded incessant travel. As his fame ascended, the travel requirement became greater than when he had played with the lesser-known shows. Success was measured in part by the number of weeks or months that a show stayed out on the road. Poor shows usually had short seasons, while the better shows experienced longer schedules.

Performers in traveling shows, minstrels, and vaudevilles measured their time on the road in two seasons. The circus season ran from March or April to November or December, and the winter season began in December and continued into March. Careful planning would provide an opportunity for perpetual work with few scheduling conflicts.

Going on the road was and remains a phrase defining the rigorous itinerant life of the traveling professional. The road also gave performers status in their home communities. This kind of travel represented the fact that someone had a special talent or ability for which a show was willing to pay. A job in the profession was a highly sought-after prize; furthermore, going on the road offered the opportunity to see exotic places and to perform for thousands in appreciative audiences. Finally, communities took particular pride in the knowledge that their performers served as unofficial representatives to the world.

The road could prove to be a hard teacher and a demanding taskmaster. It was a unique kind of survival school. There were lessons to study conscientiously and learn well. A "test" might confront the "student" at any time. Throughout a performer's career, the road demanded talent, skill, unswerving dedication, and sometimes well-being, fortunes, or, tragically, life. The tests Lowery faced included a flood, a fire, a circus robbery, windstorms, and even train wrecks.

One crucial lesson concerned an accurate evaluation of a musician's abilities when he or she applied for a job with a show. Since the society of the time generated musicians with widely varying levels of training and skills, bandleaders had to devise ways of finding musicians who would be an asset to the show. Most of the reputable shows wanted instrumentalists who were technically proficient, were capable music readers, and had the ability to "double"—to play more than one instrument well. Anxiously searching for glamorous jobs, some players would claim to have abilities that in reality they lacked. The ability to read notated music was perhaps the most widespread and recurrent false claim. Many of these players had good ears and could fake their way through a lot of the music being played. Unfortunately, however, this ruse had its drawbacks. The combination of fakers ("shammers," who could almost read and/or play) and strong musicians ("jammers") did not always provide an acceptable or even a desirable musical product for the show. According to Tom Fletcher,

When you joined a show as a musician there never was any band rehearsal. The band leader, when parade time came, would pass out the books that had all of the tunes, but with the names of the tunes cut off. The idea was to see whether you had told the truth about being a bandsman. When everyone had his book the leader would give the signal to start playing the march. [Then the leader] would get a chance to see who was cheating or wasn't a good music reader. If they were good singers and dancers the leader would let them keep their books but they would have to go off by themselves where they wouldn't disturb anyone and learn the tunes. . . .

The bands of that time usually consisted of twelve players at most. In parading, there would be ten or twelve feet between each two men. A company that could put twenty men in the street parade band would stretch further than two city blocks.[1]

Musicians playing in this kind of setting thus had to be strong players, performing as if they were soloists rather than adhering to the modern concept of ensemble playing. Unskilled players would be discovered immediately and promptly embarrassed or treated to one of many remedial options devised by the show people.

When found out, the only likely salvation for a faker would be the ability to double—dance, sing, or do something considered of value to the show. Without that, the person could endure all sorts of penalties. One very popular but not so very gentle technique was red-lighting, in which a person and sometimes his gear would be thrown off the train at any stop or even in the middle of nowhere. If the pretender was truly appalling, the show people might not wait for the train to stop. This was a dangerous practice, and show managers would not openly admit that it happened. Kinder outfits simply abandoned charlatans wherever they were discovered. This caused weaker musicians and performers to exercise extreme caution in how they answered advertisements for jobs.[2]

Another lesson taught by the road concerned establishing show connections for seeking out the right jobs. Until he became well known, Lowery played with any show that would hire him. While paying his dues, Lowery, like nearly all other performers, learned to go through a Saturday ritual: Get the *Freeman*, check the "Stage" pages to find out what shows were seeking performers, and then answer the ads. Those who were hired would later use the same sources to find out whether their employers had issued the call. Later, as Lowery's reputation developed, so did the demand for his professional services. He not only created shows for his immediate employer but also served as a development and production contractor with other road shows.

A TURN FROM MINSTRELSY

At the beginning of the 1900s, classic minstrelsy was being strongly influenced by the ongoing development of vaudeville, the Broadway stage, and other musical variations. Musicians and performers of color had begun experimenting with deviations from the usual minstrel show format that reflected what was becoming the American musical stage—theatrically oriented productions. Of these changes, Fletcher observed that as early as the 1890s, "not only was the patter of shows changed, but a new rhythm was born, and ragtime . . . songs were put on paper . . . and became the rage. Beside the 'Cake-walk,' a new dance the Pasumala, and another, the Black Annie, came into existence. These new dances were good and they enjoyed some popularity, but none of them ever surpassed, or even equaled the popularity of the Cake-walk."[3]

These "colored shows" began to develop tremendous drawing power. Managers and producers anxiously sought black talent for their many projects. Larger circuses began to feature these performances under the "white tops," circus vernacular for the sideshow tents. Three specific projects between 1890 and 1898 illustrate these changes. First, Sam T. Jack's *Creole Show* enjoyed a successful four- or five-year run near New York's Broadway beginning in 1890. Although the show was still cast in the traditional minstrel pattern, Jack was innovative in that he cast both men and women in the production.[4]

In 1895, John W. Isham, another white producer, launched *The Octoroons*, which deviated more noticeably from the minstrel format. Although very similar to the model established by the *Creole Show*, this production had a thin thread of a story and used black women in starring roles as well as in chorus numbers. In 1896, Isham offered *Oriental America*, "the first all-black show to play Broadway and the first to make a definite break with minstrel traditions. The show concluded with a medley of operatic selections, and thus demanded good singers as well as clever comedians. The stage was now set for genuine black musical comedy written and produced by blacks."[5]

In 1898, Bob Cole produced the first all-black full-length musical comedy, *A Trip to Coontown*, which also constituted the first known show written, organized, and produced by blacks. Tilford Brooks maintains that this production "broke away from the minstrel tradition by having a genuine plot, including some character development, as well as songs, dances, and pretty girls." According to Eileen Southern, "The important thing was that black-produced shows had finally succeeded in New York, the capital of the theater industry, and this breakthrough would pave the way for others." Fletcher noted that "no performer was ever satisfied until the seal of approval had been won by him in the 'Big Apple'—New York."[6]

NEWSPAPERS AND THE "HONORABLE PROFESSION"

Call was the magic word for which each performer carefully watched in the newspapers during the early spring. Calls portended recognition as a professional, and promised work during the coming season. With pride, show people would say good-bye to their homes, friends, and relations before setting off to spend another season on the road.

In the late nineteenth century, calls were made via newspapers, which often published only weekly. The papers of choice for the entertainment industry included the *Indianapolis Freeman* and some smaller journals, which regularly carried news and information of interest to the shows and the show people. The *Freeman*, the periodical of choice for African-American entertainers, was a unique newspaper that at its zenith was owned and managed by George L. Knox and his son, Elwood, who was an amateur musician and a friend of P. G. Lowery. Under the Knoxes' stewardship, the *Freeman* "moved to larger quarters in 1893 and proclaimed itself a 'national race paper.' Its profusely illustrated pages regularly included literary and historical essays, columns devoted to the interests of homemakers, farmers and mechanics, and correspondence from black communities, large and small, from Georgia to California." The Knox duo guided the paper from little more than a trade sheet to a nationally and internationally circulated publication and began to devote more ink to news of the theater and stage, sports, and other items of interest to the black communities throughout the United States.[7]

The *Freeman* developed an amazingly intricate news-gathering and circulation network, mounting nationwide subscription campaigns and soliciting advertisements from businesses and industries all over the country. To further increase circulation, the Knoxes hired as distributors

Pullman porters on the many trains running through Indianapolis and entered into similar agreements with traveling entertainers. Stage and athletic performers (including Ed Green) and blacks around the country became "special correspondents," reporting news events and items of interest. The theatrical news provided by these correspondents gave rise to a column, which evolved into a section called "The Stage" that constituted an important source of information for black actors, musicians, theatrical troupes, and various associated organizations.[8]

By consulting the *Freeman*, which came out every Saturday, readers could know where noteworthy performers were playing during the next week, how the shows were doing, who was "at liberty," and what shows were looking to hire personnel. The paper also printed gossip and offered a mailbox forwarding system through which traveling performers could receive their personal and business mail while en route."[9]

The newspaper also served in a policing capacity, printing stories regarding shady managers, poor theater conditions, and towns unfriendly to black performers. The *Freeman* demonstrated equal fervor and mercilessness against shoddy performers. The most dependable information source in African-American communities, the *Freeman* could boost or torpedo a career or a show, depending on the coverage given and reviews printed. The reporting was often very blunt and judgmental.[10] An example of the paper's wrath is indicated from an article in one of their editions entitled "A Rabbit's Foot Company Gives Bad Show." It says,

Special to The *Freeman*. Columbia, S.C., June 26.—Pat Chappel's "A Rabbit's Foot Company" was in town yesterday, and gave only one performance. The shows were simply rotten, as usual. Mack Allen, the slack wire walker, and Willie Glenn were the entire show. There are only two lady performers, and they are amateurs, and six men. Columbians did not turn out in a very large number, as they are pretty tired of Pat Chappel's Rabbit's Foot. It is given out by reliable authority that the show has spent $3,000 during the ten weeks they have been out, and are running at a great loss.[11]

The "wanted" ad was direct in its meaning, notifying all members of the profession that a company was being formed or restaffed for a coming season. Advertisers would admonish applicants to be truthful: "DO NOT MISREPRESENT, TELL WHAT YOU CAN and WILL DO, in first letter . . . don't flirt with us." Ad for the Nashville Students Company approached the point directly: "Amateurs Save Stamps!" The performance level of this and certain other shows was such that they would not accept any but the most exceptional players. There were few if any rehearsals once the show got under way, and new musicians had to produce immediately. "Wanted quick" or "at once" ads were also simplistic in wording and in meaning— a show was desperate for a performer. These announcements may have provided the best opportunities for performers trying to break into the business. Although musical and theatrical preparedness remained a necessity, as prospective employers' expectations remained high, well-prepared novices had a chance.[12]

Managers and directors would periodically run other types of ads to reach specific performers, perhaps to determine their commitments for the upcoming season. The most efficient way was through the *Freeman*. For example, in 1910, H. L. Rawles, one of Lowery's managers, published a wish list of performers for the next season, thereby subtly inquiring about their availability.[13]

The last line in most of the ads, citing the route, was most important. At the time, letters could be sent ahead to towns on the performers' itinerary, and performers would collect their mail when they arrived. Other managers and directors, including Lowery, would have their mail sent to the *Freeman* office in Indianapolis. Each issue of the paper contained the names of persons having mail at the *Freeman* office; recipients would then give forwarding instructions to the paper and would receive their mail a few days later. During the late nineteenth and early twentieth centuries, this was the model of efficiency.[14]

The *Freeman* provided crucial communications links among show people, managers, directors. It also served as a textbook and an excellent disseminator of the kind of news that was often omitted, overlooked, or inaccurately reported by other media. The *Freeman* was the circulatory system of black show business. And at the zenith of his career, Lowery's activities came to dominate the *Freeman's* show business coverage.

Newspapers also provided Lowery with a constant connection to his home. His letters to the publications became news reports, which in turn became a source of pride for the citizens of the Eureka, Kansas, area. Whatever national coverage the *Indianapolis Freeman* accorded to Lowery, the *Eureka Herald* matched on the local level. The *Herald*, therefore, published a highly accurate chronology of Lowery-related events, taken primarily from his letters to the paper. These journals thus chronicled Lowery's professional appearances and the accomplishments of his performers and shows.

AWAITING THE CALL

Lowery, not unlike other achievers, had mentors, both direct and indirect, who were instrumental in boosting the beginning of his career. His first direct mentors were perhaps his older brothers and their Star of the West Brass Band. They taught him to play his first instrument, a drum. His parents, however, were perhaps indirect contributors. Although they would not allow Perry to play the cornet inside the house, they never forbade him to play in the barn. Therefore, the people in and around Eureka were either direct or indirect mentors, providing advice, encouragement, and frequently employment over many years.

Two other people aided Lowery as his career gained momentum. His stepbrother, Edward O. Green, respected as a fine trombonist, was a show musician. Green later became Lowery's business partner, employee, and personal adviser. Green was highly regarded in the entertainment community and was once described as "another bright star in the colored profession."[15]

After several seasons on the road, Green decided to pursue a greater level of technical proficiency on his instrument by studying in Chicago. When he had completed that course of study, his teacher suggested that Green go to Boston to study with R. N. Davis, a well-known trombonist and teacher who may have been a faculty member at the New England Conservatory. Green did study at that institution.[16]

The other person who was instrumental in giving P. G. a start was his friend, George Bailey. As a veteran of the show circuit, Bailey carefully monitored Lowery's progress. Bailey had earned a good reputation, had strong performance credentials, and performed only with the better shows of the day. The *Indianapolis Freeman* said in 1897 that Bailey "has won fame by his wonderful execution and rapidity, and is also noted for his wonderful tone. As a trombone soloist, Mr. Bailey stands alone in this or any other country."[17]

As Lowery struggled along with unknown bands and hard-luck shows, Bailey mentored. Encouraging, watching, making careful suggestions, and guiding, Bailey eventually became instrumental in securing Lowery's first big job, with the Darkest America Show in the early 1890s. This launched Lowery's career in the entertainment world.

MAKING A PLACE FOR P. G.

Adam Forepaugh, a butcher and horse trader from Philadelphia, got into the circus business in 1863 "by virtue or vice of selling some horses to Pogey O'Brien, known as one of the most unscrupulous circus-show owners of the time, a 'grifter.'" Forepaugh took over the operation and developed it into a first-class show. For some time, the Adam Forepaugh Circus (often billed as "4-PAW") was the largest and finest-equipped wagon show, and it subsequently became a railroad show. On the day of President Abraham Lincoln's death, Forepaugh was taking delivery of two elephants and other animals at a cost of forty-two thousand dollars. A short time later, Forepaugh began paying a famous minstrel, Dan Rice, one thousand dollars per week to perform as a clown. Forepaugh boasted of never having had a failing season and claimed that he "owned, controlled and exhibited more wild animals and individually possessed more show property than any other person in the world." The show ran under his name from 1866 through 1890.[18]

Forepaugh died in 1890, and the Cooper and Bailey Circus took over the 4-PAW Show, operating it through the 1894 season. In 1896, James A. Bailey took over the show and combined it with "the Sells Brothers [Circus] to put out a new circus under the title 'Adam Forepaugh and Sells Brothers.' One reason Bailey did this was to furnish more competition for the rapidly growing Ringlings."[19]

The Sells Brothers—Lewis, Ephraim, Peter, and Allen—of Columbus, Ohio, owned a three-ring circus that started in 1872 under the title the Paul Silverburg Circus. In 1878, it changed from a wagon show to a railroad show using the Sells name. Although the Sells brothers were not afraid to fight any other outfit in the territorial wars, the Forepaugh–Sells Brothers combination never successfully met the Ringlings' challenge. In 1905 Bailey sold a half interest in the 4-Paw–Sells Circus to the Ringlings. A year later, the Ringlings owned the whole outfit. They operated it until 1908, temporarily retired it, and then revived it in 1910–11. After the 1911 season the Ringlings permanently retired the 4-Paw show.

Al G. Fields, who later became one of the most prominent names in minstrelsy, James Anderson, and Ben Wallace started the Great Wallace Shows in Peru, Indiana, in 1884. They enhanced the show and put it on rails in 1886. By 1887, Ben Wallace owned the whole outfit. It operated as the Cook and Whitby Circus from 1892 through 1894, when its owner renamed it the Great Wallace Circus. Through this incessant web of sales and mergers, the circus world developed a place for P. G. Lowery. Wallace had long been associated with C. H. Sweeney, who engaged in minstrel show work with both Fields and Lowery.[20]

A CHALLENGE TO THE WORLD

Lowery began working with Wallace in 1893, when he was laying the organizational groundwork for the Great Wallace Circus. Lowery left in 1894 but returned to the Wallace camp in 1898. During the winter seasons, Sweeney partnered with Lowery and subsequently managed his minstrel shows.[21]

Lowery's star began to rise around 1894, as two events sent him on his way. First, Lowery won a prestigious prize for the "finest rendered cornet solo" at the Hutchinson, Kansas, Musical Jubilee. That prize may have been a scholarship to the Boston Conservatory. According to the *Eureka Herald*, "if it was not for his color, Lowery would be probably looked upon as the peer of any living cornetist." The *Herald* quoted the *Bedford (Iowa) News* as saying, "Kansas has one of the greatest colored protégés in the person of Mr. P. G. Lowery, the cornet soloist who thrilled the city with enthusiasm.

Just think! He never took a lesson on the instrument [that] he is the master of. He has the greatest compass, the fastest execution, the sweetest tones of any cornetist that has ever visited our city, and he is a gentleman."[22]

During 1894, Perry also contracted to play a thirty-two-week engagement with a theater troupe based in Kansas City. The *Herald* reported in 1896 that Lowery ran an ad in the *New York Clipper*, a leading theatrical paper, in which he issued a "Challenge to the World": "I claim the honor of being the greatest colored cornet soloist on earth, and will meet any colored cornet soloist in a contest for a purse of from $100 to $600, said challenge expiring Aug. 1. New soloists come on or get back."[23]

The Kansas City troupe was the Nashville Students Colored Comedy Company. The name *Nashville Students* (sometimes *Nashville University Students*) was popular during the late nineteenth and early twentieth centuries for touring groups seeking to imply some kind of professional connection with Nashville's Fisk University and its popular Fisk Jubilee Singers, whose name represented quality and attracted gate receipts. Most of the "Nashville student" groups were neither from Nashville nor known to be university students.[24]

According to Doug Seroff, two companies without known connections to Nashville toured under the name "Nashville Students" in the late 1800s. The first troupe, Thearle's Nashville Students, "were based in Chicago [and] claimed to have been formed in 1879, though the earliest known references to the troupe are from the late 1880s, at which time their membership consisted almost entirely of Ohioans." This group "toured extensively in the West during the latter half of the 1890s." The second group, P. T. Wright's Nashville Students, "presented a variety program which included vocal and instrumental music, as well as comedy and dance. Their proprietor and namesake was one of a small coterie of financially successful black managers operating during the early 1890s. . . . His wife, Ida Lee Wright, of Paola, Kansas, was the 'serpentine dancer' as well as contralto with the troupe. Wright's company featured cornetist/bandmaster P. G. Lowery . . . one of the premier black musicians of the era."[25]

Preston T. Wright was born in Mexico, Missouri, in 1857 of parents owned by Quincy Daniels. After the war, the Wright family moved to

Macomb, Illinois. Preston entered the public schools there and later learned barbering. He made his first show appearance in 1874 with T. H. Bland's Carolinians, singing bass. Finding that singing was not profitable, he moved to Kansas City and became a detective (reportedly the only African-American detective in the West). Still unhappy with his lot, Wright then decided to reenter show work, putting together the Nashville Students Company with the assistance of his wife, Ida. Forty years after his birth, Wright was thought to be the most successful African-American owner-manager in the profession.[26]

The reputation of Wright's Nashville Students supported the premise that they, as an exception, were not attempting to capitalize on someone else's name. As Lowery's influence with the Students grew, he made it clear that he wanted only superlative musical talent. In 1901, for example, the announcement of the group's winter tour introduced the band, orchestra, and vaudeville troupe, which included Miss L. C. Haynes as the prima donna. Lowery specifically noted that Haynes was a music graduate of Fisk University and had sung with the London Jubilee Singers before joining Lowery's entourage.[27]

The Wright's Nashville Students 1895 touring season closed in Nauvoo, Illinois, on May 18. Lowery and Ed Green's return home was certainly newsworthy, with the *Herald* reporting that they had "arrived at their Spring Creek home last Sunday, and will remain until about August 1. . . . The boys have not decided what they will do during the coming season. They have an offer to go to Australia, with a company, this winter, and they may accept it. Mr. Lowery has few if any superiors as cornetist, and Mr. Green is equally as proficient on the slide trombone."[28] Lowery and Green stayed busy during that summer caring for the farm. As their parents aged, the sons needed to take on more farm responsibilities.

Despite their farm chores, however, the brothers' stay in Greenwood County included many musical performances for their neighbors, who apparently enjoyed these events. In mid-July, the *Herald* announced Lowery and Green's appearance at a benefit concert for the Eureka community band: "The proceeds of the concert will be applied toward the purchase of instruments and uniforms. Eureka has a good band and they are deserving of support."[29] The concert represented the continuation of twenty years of respectful competitiveness between the Lowery family's Star of the West Brass Band and the Eureka Brass Band, that had started in 1875, when Seymour Lowery challenged the Eurekans to a contest. After these contests, the Lowerys would perform with the Eureka Band and then entertain the members on the Lowery farm.

One such gathering occurred on July 27, 1895, when attendees included not only the Eureka Band but also numerous other neighbors, who were alerted to the event by an announcement in the July 26 edition of the *Herald*. The Lowerys were known far and wide as gracious hosts who could accommodate a crowd, and because the Eureka Band would not be holding its usual Saturday concert, the audience simply went to the Lowerys' affair. The party was also a farewell to Perry and Ed, who were about to leave for what the newspaper called an "Eastern Tour." On August 2, the newspaper reported that the guests

> had a very pleasant time. There was all kinds of music—instrumental, band and orchestra; vocal, quartette and solos, and the time passed too quickly. The Lowerys are royal entertainers, and the people of Reece know where to go to have a good time. Refreshments were served, consisting of cakes, ices, etc., and an abundance of good sweet cider.
>
> The singing by Gene Lowery is what "took." He is quite a good singer, and can play a tuba to perfection, for one so afflicted with "that tired feeling." The boys, Perry and Ed left Sunday night for their eastern trip. The Herald wishes for them great success.[30]

Lowery and Green were leaving Reece to begin their respective studies at the Boston and New England Conservatories.

Lowery worked vigorously during the 1895–96 season. In August 1895 he notified the people of Greenwood County via the *Herald* that he had been promoted to bandmaster of the show and that he was quite busy with this added responsibility. He was performing with the Students, studying at the Boston Conservatory under H. C. Brown, and preparing to enter yet another Kansas music contest as a cornet competitor. In conjecture, it is possible that these tasks did not always require his daily presence, and he could adjust his performance schedules in order to commute to school accordingly. In February 1896, the *Indianapolis Freeman* reported that Lowery, still traveling with the group with which he had performed for several years, was so well liked that the company gave him a gold baton and a Holton three-star Cornet, gifts valued at $125. Furthermore, the students traveled "in their own *palace* car, which cost $10,000." At around the same time, the *Herald* announced to its readers that

Mr. Perry G. Lowery, band master for the Nashville Students, has secured the finest make, the finest finished and the finest toned cornet in the world, one that was manufactured especially for him by the Boston Musical Instrument Manufacturing Company. The horn is of silver, satin finished, gold bell and keys, the latter having pearl tops. Engraved on the horn is a complete picture of his home near Reece, Kansas. This engraving is so fine and perfect that the windows, doors, fences, trees, etc., can be plainly seen. Mr. Lowery claims it to be the finest toned and easiest cornet to play he ever saw. It seems perfection in every part.

Lowery now owned at least two horns.[31]

Wright's Nashville Students pleased crowds around the country, and the group's reputation was becoming a guarantee of year-round work and money in the bank for both the show and its sponsors. In October 1895, the *Herald* reprinted a review from the *Appleton, Minnesota, Press:*

The Nashville Students and Colored Comedy Company rendered a splendid specialty program at Rink Hall Saturday evening. From their appearance on the street at noon in their attractive Zouave uniforms until the ringing down of the curtain at the close of the performance at night, they won and held the favor of the public. Prof. P. G. Lowery is a cornetist and bandmaster of more than ordinary ability, and surrounded as he was by musicians who were all soloists upon their respective instruments, his band made a decided hit. Of the performance it can be said that from the opening chorus from the opera of "Nanon" to the close of "Aunt Jane's Wooden Wedding" everything went off smoothly and elicited constant and persistent applause.[32]

In March 1896, Lowery and the Nashville Students performed at Eureka's Opera House, an event that generated much excitement on the part of the *Herald*, which eagerly announced the coming show and commented afterward on the citizens' pleasure at seeing Lowery and reiterating the great esteem in which he was held.[33]

Lowery's performances at home were always gala affairs, with many friends, relatives, and acquaintances coming out to hear his troupe. The March 1896 performances exhibited the Students' usual high degree of style and class:

The Nashville Students showed here Tuesday and Wednesday nights, and to excellent houses. This company provides an excellent entertainment, the best of the kind on the road. The members of the company are all nice people, clean in speech and action, and exceedingly able in their respective parts. And not the least clean and able are the two Greenwood County boys, who are of this company. Perry G. Lowery and E. O. Green, the former being the champion cornetist and the latter well up in G as a trombonist. Those . . . are prime favorites with our people, having spent much of their life in this county, and the fine attendance on both occasions was largely due to the regard of our people for them. [Lowery and Green] expect to be at home, Spring Creek township, in a couple of weeks for the summer.[34]

On returning home, Lowery and Green resumed their prior involvement in the local music scene. In early May, the men were on their way back to Kansas, where they were scheduled to perform in at least three programs with the Eureka Band. Much to the disappointment of the public, two appearances had to be canceled as a result of unexplained travel delays. In June, however, Lowery and Green appeared with the Eureka Band, with Lowery as the conductor. Both Green and Lowery's old friend and mentor, George Bailey, appeared as soloists under Lowery's baton, which must have made this a wonderful event for him.[35]

Later that summer, Lowery and Green gave a joint concert at the Eureka Opera House prior to their departure to join Wright's Nashville Students. Lowery had contracted for a thirty-eight week tour with the Students, which remained one of the most popular traveling companies of that time. The 1896–97 season was Lowery's third year as band director on that show. Other members of that year's troupe included J. A. Steward, tuba; M. McQuitty, baritone; Dan F. Desdunes, alto horn, composer, and orchestra leader; L. E. Gideon, cornet; F. C. Richardson, clarinet; Harry Gilliam, alto horn; Ed McGruder, trombone; A. P. Harris and Gordon C. Collins, percussions; and Bessie Gilliam and Ida Lee Wright, singers.[36]

During his travels, Lowery periodically corresponded with both the *Herald* and the *Freeman* to describe his troupe's progress and accomplishments. In October 1896, the *Herald* reported that Lowery had written from Clearfield, Iowa, on September 29, "I am getting along O.K., I like my position. The show was a good one this year. I am leading a good all K. [nights] of P. [ythias] band and I am well pleased with it. My cornet playing is a decided hit this year. I have played before such critics as Leberati, Prof. Landers and others, and won him thoroughly." Lowery also stated that he was planning a brief visit to Reece on November 29 while en route to an appearance in Wichita a day later. The *Herald* also shared with its readers a report from the *Topeka Capital* that Lowery "has become a member of Jackson's Band, in Topeka. Perry will however, remain on the road during the rest of the season. Jackson's Band is the leading colored band in the state and has a membership of fifty."[37]

The Students show continued, and their season never seemed to end. The rapidly deteriorating health of Lowery's father, Andrew, caused P. G. and Ed Green to interrupt their tour and make several trips home. The two stayed in Reece from late February until March 4, when they left to catch up to the show at Chillicothe, Missouri. During this visit home, Seymour Lowery also returned to see his father as well as Seymour and P. G.'s sister, Nettie Wright. P. G. and Ed were expected to return home again in mid-May.[38]

SUMMER SCHOOL

During a time off from the Students in the 1897 season, Lowery and Green completed significant portions of their courses of study at the Boston and New England Conservatories. They were clearly very positive about their professional training and had been "assured by the master critics that each of them possessed natural ability, and that, under careful training, such as they would receive, would become proficient performers on their respective instruments, cornet and trombone; in fact, would themselves soon become teachers and critics, not only as related to the cornet and trombone, but of the entire family of band instruments." The end of their studies was in sight, and they wanted the people at home to know of their achievements. On June 11, the *Herald* published an item stating that the paper had received a letter from Lowery in which he reported that he and his brother "expect to finish their course early in the fall, when they return home. They promise their Greenwood county friends an opportunity for hearing them. The boys have none but friends in Greenwood, and all will greatly rejoice to learn of their success. Their ambition to become proficient musicians is a commendable one, and our people are proud of them." Near the end of their break, Lowery and Green did return home.[39]

RETURN TO THE STUDENTS

After this brief hiatus, Lowery and Green returned to Wright's Nashville Students, a show whose reputation had remained consistently high. The show's return to Eureka in December 1897 was flat, however, with the exception of the instrumental department. According to the *Herald*,

P. T. Wright's Nashville Students and Concert Company played for a hundred dollar house at the opera house Friday night. Their show was fair. Some was good, and some bad. The band and orchestra was good, being the best carried by the company. All are musicians and their playing won much applause. P. G. Lowery and E. O. Green, the Eureka boys with the company, since their studies at the Boston conservatory, have improved considerable and are considered by all who attended the show the best talent Mr. Wright carries. Mr. Lowery's cornet solos received great applause, and they deserved it. Outside the instrumental music the show was not up to expectations. Heretofore the company has carried several excellent singers. This time, with possibly a couple of exceptions, they were lacking. Entirely too much time was wasted in vulgarity and stale fun. If Mr. Wright will bring that part of the show up to the standard maintained in the band and orchestra, he will be deserving of the claim of a first class company.[40]

The flatness of the Eureka show was apparently an aberration. Consistently poor shows usually came off the road after a few weeks, but the Nashville Students played on.

As in the majority of these traveling shows, most people did double duty. J. A. Stewart, the tuba player, was also the slack-wire artist. Stewart and his wife, Anna, also performed a comedy sketch called "The Night before the Circus." Ida Lee Wright sang and danced and served as the company's treasurer. Harry Gilliam served as the stage manager, and his wife, Bessie, sang and did acrobatics. Drummer Gordon Collins sang as well. In addition to his managerial duties, P. T. Wright was a bass singer/soloist.[41]

By February 1898, the Students had been on the road since August 15 of the previous year without a close, and they were booked solid through June in Tennessee, Arkansas, Missouri, Kentucky, Illinois, Ohio, Wisconsin, Nebraska, and Iowa. During their tour of Tennessee, they began to receive fan mail that they shared with the *Freeman*. Ben M. Stainback, the manager of a Memphis venue, wrote to Lowery that "After booking the Nashville Students I was afraid I was up against it, but I assure you I was agreeably surprised in their performance, especially in their band work under your leadership, and more especially was I delighted with your cornet solo work on the stage. Many of my patrons declared you could not be beat and, believe me, I never heard better work on that instrument and I have had all of the big bands on my stage." Of the Students' Memphis performance, the local paper reported that "The Nashville Students Concert Band under the leadership of P. G. Lowery, the greatest of all cornet soloists, is the only colored band that ever concerted in Memphis, and the music rendered defied criticism." The *Nashville Evening Journal* said that "The Streets of Nashville were crowded to hear a special concert at 7 o'clock by the crack band of artists under the leadership of P. G. Lowery. Special mention is due Messers L. E. Gideon, Dan Desdunes, E. O. Greene, M. M. McQuitty and John Stewart, the five soloists, who were competing for public honors. They were crowned with rounds of applause."[42]

Just when the company seemed to have arrived at the pinnacle of achievement, tragedy struck. At the beginning of March 1898, P. T. Wright became ill, and he died on March 15 in Cincinnati. After Wright's death, his widow kept the show going, meeting all of its commitments. Lowery became the manager, and the show retained its high level of quality. Ida Lee Wright also made some adjustments to the cast, including adding a "gun manipulator," or trick-shot artist, who was a hit with the audiences and with the other performers. Of the troupe's March 23 performance in Delphi, Indiana, the *Freeman* reported,

The playing of the band itself was remarkably good, the two productions were solid and smooth and the phrasing admirable. Great vigor, dash and enthusiasm was conspicuous indeed. I can only say who[ever] missed hearing this band missed a tremendously and unusual[ly] good thing. I cannot close without a few direct remarks for Prof. P. G. Lowery, cornet soloist and leader of the band, your playing is remarkable for its simple and singular purity. The tones you produced are clear and well sustained and true to nature in their bird-like clearness [and] execution . . . betray the marks of a master performer.[43]

Between 1890 and 1905, Lowery became recognized as the preeminent show bandleader. His bands were beginning to demonstrate a unique quality that many other ensembles desired. The repertoire included a wide range of musical styles, from operatic overtures and marches to popular music. Other bands began to copy his style.

At the end of June 1898, Lowery left the Nashville Students and went to Omaha, Nebraska, to perform at the Trans-Mississippi Exposition. His departure from the Students was apparently amicable, and the careers of both Lowery and the Students continued to meet with great success.[44]

THE 1898 OMAHA EXPOSITION

The Trans-Mississippi and International Exposition, the formal name of the 1898 Omaha Exposition, was a spectacular undertaking for its time, second in elaborateness only to a previous World's Fair, the 1893 Chicago Columbian Exposition. The Trans-Mississippi Exposition included a midway, unique architecture, items representing the latest technical advances, and thousands of exhibits. As exhibitors applied finishing touches prior to the opening, "the scene on the grounds is one of bustling activity. . . . On the midway are some strange looking people who will presently occupy the different villages. The quaint looking buildings, with their foreign, unfamiliar architecture, are nearly completed. A Japanese tea garden, a Moorish village, with an intervening court filled with shady trees, a giant iron seesaw, Germans, Chinese and Negro villages with their typical accessories, great pavilions, odd little nooks and corners go to make up a most attractive looking amusement quarter."[45]

The formal opening ceremony on June 1 demonstrated the level of grandeur that the exposition would present. Preceded by a midmorning parade, the opening ceremony included musical performances by the U.S. Marine Corps Band, the 150-member Trans-Mississippi Exposition Chorus, and Theodore Thomas's Chicago Orchestra. The ceremony culminated with President William McKinley touching "a button in Washington which . . . set in motion the machinery of the Trans-Mississippi Exposition at Omaha. Previous to starting the machinery, the President [spoke] a few words of greetings over the long distance telephone. The message [was then] read to the audience by Governor Silas A. Hedgecomb of Nebraska." The evening featured a Grand Opening Concert and a giant fireworks display.[46]

Lowery's "remarkable" cornet solos were well received by exposition audiences, and the *Indianapolis Freeman* called him "the pride of the Trans-Mississippi Exposition," possessing a "phenomenal range on the cornet." Lowery was genuinely amazed, however, when he was advised that "all first-class musicians recognize[d] his tones on the cornet for four blocks distant."[47]

While at the exposition, Lowery engaged in a full-scale musical competition, or "cutting match," with another highly regarded African-American cornetist, W. C. Handy. Born in 1873, in Florence, Alabama, William Christopher Handy was raised in a strictly religious household in which his father, a minister, and mother believed that all music except sacred music was sinful. When the young Handy saved up his money and purchased a guitar, his outraged father insisted that this "devil's plaything" be returned to the store and exchanged for a dictionary. Despite his obvious musical aptitude, Handy's parents strongly attempted to persuade their son to pursue other vocational interests, preferably the ministry.[48]

Both Handy and Lowery were driven from within to further their musical careers, and their paths would intersect. Handy worked his way up through the ranks to became the director of W. A. Mahara's Minstrel Show Band, and by 1897, he was "making quite a reputation as a cornet soloist"— and becoming aware of Lowery's existence. In his autobiography, Handy described how he first noticed Lowery around 1896, following "along behind

our band in Council Bluffs, Iowa. He was a dark, handsome man, but noticeably shy and bent on attracting as little attention as possible. I couldn't imagine what he was up to. No words were exchanged. He simply followed,
watching and listening intently, as if he had been employed to shadow me."[49]

Handy and Lowery again encountered each other at the Trans-
Mississippi Exposition, where Lowery was performing as the featured cornet
soloist. There, Handy saw Lowery "blowing . . . as to suggest that he might
have been Gabriel's right-hand man." One evening, after Lowery's exposition performance, some of the musicians from Handy's minstrel show
instigated a musical contest of skills between Lowery and Handy by invit-
ing Lowery to the Mahara show site. He quietly accepted. Such contests
were commonplace among bands on the road, but the Mahara musicians
obviously thought that Handy, the virtuoso, would easily outplay Lowery,
despite his superb skills.[50]

As Handy's band members had intended, the session quickly evolved
into an intense, relentless, full-blown musical cutting match, with each
musician doing his absolute best to outplay ("blow away") the other.
Handy held his own but could not prevail. As he described the event, "We
got together and took each other's measure like a pair of gamecocks in a
crowing match. I called for a number, and he gave it to me with plenty of
gravy and dressing. He named his terms, and I came back with my Sunday
best. From that day, my great[est] ambition was to outplay P. G."[51]

After the dust of battle had settled, Lowery, in his usual style, extended
a hand of friendship to his colleague. Handy likely flashed his trademark,
a winning smile, in return. The two great musicians held each other in
the highest esteem throughout the remainder of their individual careers.
There is no record that either man harbored personal or professional ani-
mosity toward the other, and Handy and Lowery continually spoke well
of each other. According to Handy, in 1899, Lowery told the *Freeman* that
"W. C. Handy's street work is smooth, his triple tonguing is brilliant and
he certainly plays a song to suit me." Handy appreciated the compliment
but claimed that "P. G. was being overgenerous. The palm was his."[52]

After completing his engagement at the Trans-Mississippi Exposition in
late September 1898, Lowery became a special soloist at the Moorish Cafe in

Omaha, where he was reportedly "the only colored artist ever engaged." His appearance there was interrupted by the illness of his father, and on November 5, the *Freeman* reported that Lowery "is now band director of J. E. George's Concert Band, where he states, was found a lot of first-class musicians, which will be ready to meet any band of its size, regardless of color."[53]

LOWERY'S NEW GEORGIA MINSTREL BAND

J. E. George's Concert Band toured with a troupe called the Georgia Up-to-Date Minstrel Company. The phrase *Georgia Minstrels* indicated companies made up of black performers, and the phrase *Up-to-Date* distinguished this group from other companies of Georgia Minstrels.[54]

From this association, the concept of a P. G. Lowery band began to emerge and draw notice. In this forum, he could interject his ideas on performance skills and techniques. In November 1898, the *Freeman* noted that Lowery "is scoring a big hit with his concert band with the Georgia Up-to-Date." Two weeks later, the paper announced, "Lowery will soon add three more musicians to his concert band with George's Operatic Minstrels. As a director, Mr. Lowery is meeting with equal success as his cornet solo work." And in early December, the *Freeman* commented, "As a cornet soloist, Mr. Lowery's playing is remarkable for its limpid and singular purity. His triple-tongue and execution is equal to any of the leading white soloists of the country."[55]

Lowery awed his audiences with the style and dignity he brought to his performances. There was indeed something unique about Lowery that set his playing apart from that of the many other cornetists of that day. Lee Collins, a performer who heard Lowery play later in his career, described the experience as a "thrill": He could make C over high C like it was nothing at all; he was the greatest of all time. The way he blew made goose pimples come over me; I had never heard a cornet player like him in my life before. I do know that it was a great thing for all the musicians to listen to Lowery."[56]

By Christmas of 1898, it was obvious that the Georgia Minstrels' show was developing a good business reputation. There were no signs of a schedule break. Lowery had adjusted well to his new company, and on one occasion, "the band boys surprised him at band rehearsal by presenting him a large collection of the latest and [most] choice band music." The Georgia Up-to-Date spent three cold winter weeks in Minnesota, playing to standing-room-only audiences. The *Freeman* shared with its readers a detailed description of the program:

The show opens with an overture entitled "Little Harry," arranged by Harry Gilliam which never fails to start the show going. . . . The ladies of the company deserve special mention. They display great taste in their songs, dances and specialty work.

The olio opens with P. G. Lowery the great cornet soloist, which never fails to start the wheel rolling nicely, followed by the Woods, Fountain B. and Carrie in songs, trombone solos and cake walking specialty which never fails to catch. Jack M. Oliver in his monologue and parody singing is exceedingly clever and never fails to receive three and four encores nightly. The Gilliams, Harry L. and Bessie, they never fail to leave the audiences hollowing for more. Julius Glenn and A. T. Gilliam close the olio in their new act, entitled "Zizz," which keeps the people in an uproar from the time they enter until they beg permission from the audience to let them go.

Then comes the 48 minute last act entitled "Georgia Up-to-Date." Much credit is due the author Mr. Jack Oliver. The feature of the last act is a song and dance by three of the leading ladies: Miss Bessie Gilliam, Miss Nettie Titus, and Miss Carrie B. Wood. Everything is running nicely and the gentleman in white [the paymaster] appears every Sunday.[57]

By January 1899, the band was billed as "P. G. Lowery's Famous Concert Band with the Georgia Up-to-Date Minstrels." A January 7 review in the *Freeman* stated that there were no words to describe the excellence of a concert in Grand Forks, North Dakota, that lasted two hours and fifteen minutes and resulted in thunderous ovations from the audience. According to the *Freeman*, Lowery was so pleased with this performance that he spoke to his band after the show:

Gentlemen of the band, words are inadequate to express to you, as my highly esteemed band the honor and credit that was shown to us by the hearty applause that followed every number on the program tonight. My selected soloists for the occasion, Mr. Joe Pleasant, Fountain Wood, Harry L. Gilliam, and S. H. Lane displayed great taste in the rendition of their solos. Special mention is due Mr. Gilliam in the perfect rendition of his alto solo. Being of a song style, your tones produced were broad, bright, well sustained with careful breath control and perfect attack. The tuba solo rendered by Mr. Pleasant showed he was a master of his instrument. In regards to Mr. Wood I wish to say without flattery, your future as a trombone soloist is bright. You have a good tone, rapid execution and power. With your ambition, you rank with the leading trombone soloists of the day. My clarinet soloist Mr. H. S. Lane played smooth, even and distinct. In regard to my cornet section Mr. J. T. Lewis, Wm. Malone and Jeff Smith, your unison passages were just like one with good power at the end of my baton.[58]

As the Lowery name became ever more widely recognized, P. G. did not forget the people who had helped him in his developing professional career. The *Freeman* noted in March 1899 that George Bailey, who had helped Lowery secure his first show jobs, "was the recipient of a handsomely engraved medal from Prof. P. G. Lowery of the Georgia Up-to-Date Company."[59]

In the spring of 1899, L. E. Gideon, who was serving as the manager of the Nashville Students Company, visited Lowery and the Georgia Up-to-Date in Des Moines, Iowa. The *Indianapolis Freeman* reported that "The Nashville Students, the Georgia Up-to-Date and the famous Canadian Jubilee Singers spent Easter Sunday in Des Moines, Iowa. It was one of the jolliest meetings in the history of the three companies. . . . The two bands . . . united in a consolidated concert under the direction of P. G. Lowery." Shortly thereafter, in April 1899, Lowery closed with the Georgia Up-to-Date Show and then took a short break.[60]

FOREPAUGH, SELLS BROTHERS, AND THE NASHVILLE STUDENTS IN UNISON

Territorial battles were raging among the Ringlings, the Sells Brothers, James A. Bailey, and other circus operators. Some shows at times reaped windfalls out of the chaos, while others got nothing. Some shows made money, while others simply did not.

Opening the season for New York's Madison Square Garden brought great financial and morale advantages to a circus. Bailey had first done so, but Adam Forepaugh had usurped that glory. To save face in what was apparently an embarrassing situation, Bailey struck a deal to begin combining his show with Forepaugh's in the Garden each year, resulting in a grand spectacle that included sixty elephants and a host of other elements. This move also blocked other shows from premiering at the Garden each season. Later, when Bailey took over the 4-PAW Show, he combined his production with that of the Sells Brothers, seeking to challenge the Ringlings, who were also growing in competitive stature. The Ringling show fiercely battled the Bailey operation for territory at every turn, with each doing its best to one-up its competitors. New acts were contracted, some old attractions were discontinued, and millions of dollars changed hands.

Entering this array of mammoth productions in 1899 came P. G. Lowery with his sideshow minstrel performers and his band, which joined the Forepaugh and Sells Brothers Circus, opening the season at Madison Square Garden with a gala that included a huge street parade. The combined show concept apparently worked in favor of Bailey and the 4-PAW–Sells operation. Reporting on this inaugural performance, the *Indianapolis Freeman* stated, "The Forepaugh and Sells Brothers' Circus, which opened at the Garden last night, scored a big hit. A great many people who attended the opening feared that it wouldn't be as good as Barnum's, but it stood comparison with the greatest show on earth and came through with flying colors."[61]

The *Freeman* reported as early as February that Lowery was looking forward to having a first-class concert band for the summer season. He was busily searching for the country's best talent to include in his new show. Lowery began organizing his entourage in April 1899 following a call that appeared in the *Freeman* beginning on April 8. The call announced that all persons booked with Lowery were to report to Julius Glenn, stage manager, in Brooklyn, New York, by April 27. Lowery's work then began again in earnest, since organizing, training, and overseeing the day-to-day preparations for putting a show on the road was a demanding task.[62]

Lowery emphasized not only talent but also costuming, sets, and the environment in which these performers would make their presentations. Lowery is recognized as having modernized the sideshow presentation into a full-fledged after-show performance. In 1910, the *Freeman* recalled,

The Branch of the colored show business known as circus minstrels and vaudeville had its beginnings with P. G. Lowery, the renowned cornetist and bandmaster. This was at Madison Square Garden, New York, in 1899, with Sells and Forepaugh Circus. Previous to that time, the colored department consisted of a band of eight pieces, seated like the circus blues.

At present, every company has a large stage, where there are nicely covered chairs, presenting a neat and attractive appearance. This helps both the audience in appreciating and also helps the performers, who do better work under better conditions.

Since Lowery's initiative all have fallen in line—the little [shows] and the big ones—until at this time, no less than fourteen white tents are giving employment to big colored companies. P. G. Lowery's company has always numbered from eighteen to twenty-two people.

Lowery has the best company of the kind before the public; it consists of minstrel, band and orchestra, the best he has ever had.[63]

This 1899 season kicked off a stellar relationship between Lowery's organization and the 4-PAW and Sells Brothers Circus, including changes of names and management, that lasted until after the 1911 season.

The show opened with a band of twelve musicians and six specialty people—singers, dancers, comedians, and so forth—plus Julius Glenn, the stage manager and cakewalk specialist. The cakewalk, a combination of high-stepping dance and grand march led by Glenn and several beautiful women, was the highlight of the afternoon concerts. High turnover among performers was not uncommon. After the season opening, James White, a comedian and performer, joined the company. As the show traveled north to Montreal, Canada, Mr. and Mrs. Skip Farrell, a drummer and soubrette (an attractive female singer, dancer, and actress), signed on. William May, a well-known tuba player, then joined the band in Indianapolis. While playing Kansas City, Mr. and Mrs. Thomas J. Lewis—he a conductor and cornetist and she a soubrette and cornetist—joined the show. The Lewises had previously worked with Lowery on the Georgia Up-to-Date Minstrels Show. In Kansas City, James Taylor, a tenor soloist, joined the entourage. The last additions were Mr. and Mrs. Prentis Oliver, specialty performers who sang the latest "coon songs." William Malone, the orchestra leader, left and was replaced by a "Mr. Jones of Elmira, New York." Tuba player Joe Pleasant left in Indianapolis to join with Richard and Pringle, Rusco and Holland's Big Minstrel Festival. Allie T. Gilliam took charge of the stage management and cakewalk, replacing Glenn, who left at Logansport, Indiana, to join Richards and Pringle. Glenn was also a drummer, and C. W. Gossett, a trap drummer from Wichita, Kansas, finished the season after Glenn's departure. The four women who remained with the show at the end of the season were Bessie Gilliam, Tina Mazelle, Mrs. Prentis Oliver and Mrs. T. J. Lewis.[64]

In July 1899, four months after Gideon visited Lowery and the Georgia Up-to-Date Minstrel Company, the *Freeman* stated that "Misses Edna King and Bessie Gilliam and Messers M. McQuitty, Jeff Smith and Skip Farrell were callers at the *Freeman* Office this week. These ladies and gentlemen are members of P. G. Lowery's Nashville Students and Famous Concert Band." The article further noted that Lowery's Famous Concert Band and the Nashville Students show were making a big hit wherever they appeared with the Forepaugh–Sells Brothers Circus.[65]

The exact details of Lowery and Gideon's transaction are unknown. Several scenarios, however, might have brought about Lowery's reunion with the Nashville students. One possibility is that Lowery had invested heavily in the development of P. T. Wright's Nashville Students before leaving the show to perform in Omaha, and Lowery now had the established financial backing of the Forepaugh–Sells combine and the managerial authority to secure talent according to his own specifications. Another possibility is that during this period of show warfare, the Students' year-round show found itself in serious financial trouble, like many other small companies that faced no choice but to declare bankruptcy.

The 4-PAW and Sells Brothers Circus closed its 1899 season on November 18 in Alexandria, Louisiana, bringing to an end an almost seven-month season, an extremely long tenure for a circus at the time. Some of the other shows, both large and small, that had opened the season in April were back home, or "at liberty," three weeks later, casualties in the still-smoldering circus wars. Lowery's sideshow performers played a prominent role in the assurance of this successful season.[66]

At the closing of the circus season, which also marked the opening of the theater season, some performers left Lowery's operation to work with other shows. This practice was not unusual, and it did not necessarily indicate a bad experience with the company. Performers often contracted with one show for the circus season and with a second show for the theater season.

At the end of the season, Lowery sent a report to the *Freeman* in which he extended his "sincere thanks to each and every member of [the] company for their diligent work and excellent conduct, which I owe much to them for sustained reputation as director and manager. I must thank the *Freeman* for its support and prestige it has given me. To my company, I extend through the columns of the *Freeman*, a cheerful good-bye until we meet in Madison Square Garden, New York City."[67]

By December 1899, Lowery was trouping again, this time with an entourage called the Original Nashville Students combined with Lowery and Green's Improved Minstrels. Apparently doing good business, the group was reported to be twenty-five strong, including Lowery; Perkins and Chapman, comedians and buck-and-wing dancers; Harry L. Gilliam, a "great acrobatic Hebrew comedian;" Madame Hattie Lucas, soprano vocalist; Allie Gilliam and Tina Mazelle, up-to-date sketches; Arthur Prince, a slack-wire artist and juggler; and Ella Dorsey, a contortionist.[68]

January 1900 found Lowery hard at work as a performer and as a show operator, planning for his coming season of vaudeville shows and the concert band with Forepaugh-Sells. He projected a larger band, a much stronger vaudeville, and the addition of a specialty quartet of female singers as well as a male quartet. He also authored an article that appeared the *Freeman*. Entitled "The Cornet and Cornetists of To-Day," this piece was unique for its time in that he diplomatically and objectively critiqued the leading cornetists of the day, his colleagues and competitors. His article also imparted pedagogical values, recommended technical studies, and provided encouragement for aspiring cornetists and band directors. Although he addressed others, he also described his own musical-development techniques and preparation.

Since leaving Boston two years ago, I have received numerous letters from ambitious cornetists and aspiring band masters, asking my candid opinion of our present cornetists and bandmasters of the present. . . .

As this is a very important question and the honor is bestowed on me, I will endeavor to deal justly and be honest in my remarks concerning the different cornetists and bandmasters I have chanced to meet in the past two years.

The cornet [is] without a doubt, a lifetime study, possessing more points of study than any instrument in the brass family. An artist must accomplish all of these different points in equality. So there are very few artists among us. I will name a few points most absolutely necessary to observe and cultivate in order to become a thorough cornetist, namely position, tone, breath control, attack and equal balance in four different styles of tonguing, vocal connection and the natural gift of phrasing which cannot be taught. . . .

To master the cornet the most important point is to know the instrument. One must know their own weakness; know what to practice; how to practice and when to advance. If the balance of tone is neglected the quality of music is bad, no matter how perfect the other points may be. This fault is caused by stopping the tone with the tongue and not discerning the difference between the quarters, eighths and sixteenth notes and rests likewise.

There are many cornetists possessing wonderful skill on the cornet, and presume there are many more I have not met and I will venture to say several I have not heard of, whose future is bright and will some day stand out as stars in the profession.

Special compliments is due several of our leading cornetists as their improvements marks careful practice. I will set the pace by presenting Mr. Harry Prampin, the noted little bandmaster and cornetist. His position is in keeping with good taste and comfort, his tones are rich and large, especially in the lower register of the instrument where the foundation of the tone is based; his pedal tones are broad, distinct and in perfect time, and he obtains them in a perfect lip position; and with the same ease he does the middle tones. I must say in this one point he excels all others, and as a business cornetist he is on top.

Where on the other hand Elmore Dodd another hard worker, without a single doubt excels in the upper register of the instrument; his high tones are simply wonderful, broad, clear, bright and full, even above the imagination of all comers. In his solo work he wears an air of confidence that impresses his hearers to wait for the final and be convinced. At a distance one would scarcely believe the tones were from an E^b cornet.

Another example, I take pleasure in presenting and that is my friend, Wm. Handy. I feel safe in saying he deserves more credit than is dealt to him. His street work is very brilliant (but not blasty); his orchestra work is smooth and tasty and he certainly plays a song to suit me. . . .

As a business cornetist I can justly head that list with Mr. Joe Dobbins, Chicago's favorite. I find quite an interesting class of business players. We have N. R. Walker, of Boston; A. H. Montgomery of N. Y. City, Eugene McDonald, of St. Louis and Buddie Robinson of Chicago and several others that space will not allow me to mention. In this class of workers we will find some of our most thorough cornetists, because they must be well up in their different points to hold their place. Although they are not posing as soloists they can give justice to most any of the standard solos.

We have a younger class of cornetists who are climbing the ladder with unquestionable rapidity and with proper training in the technical points on the cornet. I can see in the future less room on top. The honor of the class falls to—well it is hard to say, but my mind prompts me to name Geo. Bryant of Prampin's Concert Band, J. J. Smith my pupil and also James Wilson, the brilliant little cornetist with the Nashville Students Band No. 2. From you boys, I expect a great harvest. . . .

I am proud to note such advancement in the work of our leading band masters. Henderson Smith, James Lacy and R. N. Thompson have set the pace for us. It is not absolutely necessary to play every instrument in the band to be a good director but one must know the requirements of the different instruments. . . .

I attribute the success of my band to private training. All band masters [should] know the possibilities of each member of his band and select music within the limit of their ability. In conclusion as we are about to take one more step from the old year to the new let us start with renewed vigor; let us march hand in hand and throw off all appearance of malice and back-biting and as we reach the top we must work hard to hold our place. We must constantly produce something new to attract the attention of those below us.[69]

Through his music and now also his journalism, Lowery had definitely developed a following by the dawn of the twentieth century.

Among the stops that Lowery's troupe made that winter was a February date in Eureka. The *Eureka Herald* reported,

The opera house was packed to receive the Nashville Students Saturday night, and every one seemed to thoroughly enjoy the entertainment. There were many new and novel features, but the number that captivated the audience was P. G. Lowery's cornet solo. He was repeatedly encored. . . . Lowery and Green are the owners of the Nashville Students Company. Lowery is leader of the band and director of the concert, and Green is the business manager. They have been in this business about eight years and have been very successful. . . . They both say that they love Greenwood county and its people and that they will never forget the kindness shown them whenever they visit their old home.[70]

The Forepaugh and Sells Brothers Circus, which used the billing "The Greatest Show on Earth" before the Ringlings did, opened the 1900 season in New York's Madison Square Garden, playing to good houses there from April 4 through April 21. The show then moved on to play Baltimore on April 23 and 24, and the *Indianapolis Freeman* reported that Lowery had the "largest bandwagon on parade," a spectacular vehicle painted a brilliant blue with gold trim, matching the band's uniforms, which were dark blue trimmed with gold braid. In addition, "every department is much larger this season. Lowery opened with a band of 14, orchestra of 8, a lady quartette and Mr. William Sherrah's Quartette from Kansas City, Mo., making a company of 22 people."[71]

But something happened at this point that severed Lowery and Green's association. The *Freeman* reported simply that "P. G. Lowery is not connected with Lowery and Green's Minstrels. All mail will reach him by address to the *Freeman* Office."[72] No further details concerning this startling announcement have been discovered.

From the April 23rd opening in Baltimore, Lowery's season with 4-PAW was apparently a very productive one. They played for one week in Boston wherein the "stars" of the sideshow included: singer Mrs. Nettie Lewis; the comedian and stage manager A. T. Gilliam; drummer Skip and singer Edna Farrell; the Sherrah Quartet; and P. G. Lowery.[73] Socially the company was feted with several affairs, including a "royal reception" at the home of the showman Cal Towers in Muscatine, Iowa,[74] a banquet and ball given them by the Tuxedo Club in Omaha,[75] and other receptions which Lowery states "are too numerous to mention."[76]

The show continued to mount a record of triumph through their closing date on November 3, 1900 in Aberdeen, Mississippi. Lowery called ". . . particular attention to the uncommon fact that speaks highly in favor for a successful season for any company that is that 22 members that consist my band, orchestra and vaudeville show that hear[d] the bugle sound April 23, in Baltimore, all are here to shake hands and bid God's speed."[77]

LOWERY'S PROGRESSIVE MUSICAL ENTERPRISE

In January 1901, the *Eureka Herald* announced that Lowery had become "assistant manager of W. I. Swain's original Nashville Students, and . . . conductor of what is known as P. G. Lowery's world famous colored concert band. During the summer seasons he has a position as band director for Four Paws and Sells Shows."[1] Lowery was an astute businessman, and he began to make changes in his shows according to the dictates of the times and what appeared to be popular demand. The term *vaudeville* was replacing *minstrel* as the expression of choice for these units, and Lowery's press releases began to refer to his organization as P. G. Lowery's Concert Band and Vaudeville Show or Company.[2] He would open his season with the 4-Paw at Madison Square Garden and continue to sharpen his acts as they traveled across the country each season.

Lowery's show repertoire began to include the increasingly popular ragtime music. Writing to the *Freeman*, Lowery acknowledged that "it is a great pleasure for me to state that the late composition by Scott Joplin, 'A Breeze from Alabama' is a hit everywhere. It is fast growing popular."[3]

Lowery was impressed by Joplin's music and increasingly performed his compositions, and the two men developed great respect for each other. According to Edward A. Berlin, during 1901 the *Indianapolis Freeman* began to print Lowery's praise of Joplin's work, and it "is evident that Joplin and Lowery were friends. Aside from the good notices, Lowery visited Joplin in November [1901]." During his 1901 tour with the Forepaugh and Sells Brothers Circus, Lowery featured himself performing Joplin's "Sunflower Slow Drag" in addition to the usual band songs and classical transcriptions. In October 1902, the *Freeman* reported that an audience was spellbound when it heard "the latest of Scott Joplin's rags . . . 'A Breeze from Alabama,' dedicated to P. G. Lowery."[4]

Lowery's relationship with Joplin also came to include marketing endorsements. In addition to respect for Lowery's musical skills, Joplin and his publisher, John Stark, had developed sufficient marketing expertise to recognize that for their ragtime sheet music to sell, it had to be maintained in a cloak of middle-class propriety. Stark therefore

avoided vulgar, demeaning illustrations on the covers of Joplin compositions in favor of straightforward, sometimes elegant designs. In these ways, Stark and Joplin hoped to convince consumers that Joplin's style of ragtime was respectable.

Some covers included cameo photographs of the composer . . . or people to whom a piece was dedicated, like P. G. Lowery, touted as the "World Challenging Colored Cornetist and Band Master."[5]

In April 1902, Lowery performed at New York's Douglas Club in New York, apparently just before opening with the Forepaugh–Sells Circus in Madison Square Garden. After a vaudeville performance, the "musical program rendered by P. G. Lowery's Band was excellent. Each number was responded to generously. The cornet solos of P. G. Lowery clearly proved to the audience that he is master of the instrument. . . . After the band concert, the hall was cleared and dancing followed until the hour of five." The vaudeville orientation was to become an integral part of the sideshow this season. The *Freeman* reported that Lowery's show was larger, and the band included J. J. Smith, Thomas May, Wilfred H. Day, George P. Hambright, Wilbur

Sweatman, Henry Rawles, John P. Jones, James Hall, James Morton, Fred W. Simpson, William May, Samuel Elliott, and Charles Foster. Sweatman held the dual roles of clarinetist with the band and violinist and orchestra leader.

Sweatman's infectious clarinet style excited the crowds. According to Tom Fletcher, "there would be a street parade the night before the opening [of the circus], with bands, animals, actors, clowns, everything except the freaks. The colored band made the parade in New York and . . . the crowd that lined the side walks started following the band just to hear Sweatman playing his clarinet. Everybody was saying that they had never heard anybody play the instrument like that before. Sweatman was the sensation of the parade."[6]

Lowery's next new feature was a vocal group called the Four-in-Hand Quartet that included Ambrose Davis, William Johnson, Arthur Wilmore, and Jack Watkins. Lowery also did not miss the current emphasis on beautiful women: according to the *Freeman*, "too much cannot be said of the ladies, they are good looking, good dressers, well behaved and are clever performers. Everybody knows Miss Sallie Lee, formerly of the Octroon Company. Miss Essie Williams is with [the show] this season and also adds greatly to both the appearance and value of the company. Miss Gracie Hoyt from N.Y. has made many friends by her earnest work. In fact, everybody is stuck on [the] girls."[7]

Many of the performers also had business responsibilities. Lowery served as band manager and director, Smith was assistant band director, Sweatman was orchestra director, Davis was stage manager, Foster was assistant stage manager, Morton was librarian, and Lee was agent for the *Freeman*.[8]

Lowery's show had a great season. In Baltimore, the troupe performed for more than nine thousand people, a spectacular audience described in the show vernacular as "doing good business." The tour included outside performances and social events along with the routine circus work. Lowery's band presented a special concert in Washington, D.C., for a man named Cooper who edited a newspaper called the *Colored American*. According to the *Freeman*, the company members were well and happy on this tour.[9]

In addition to dealing with the current circus tour, Lowery was planning for the coming winter season, seeking personnel and arranging music and programs. He continued the development of his show style and image. In 1903 Lowery purchased a first-class show car for the substantial sum of one thousand dollars. With three business associates, he intended to turn out the Nashville Students in all their glory. In addition, he had progressively turned their production from that of a pure minstrel show into a "three-act musical comedy, portraying the colored man from slavery to the present."[10]

FORMATION OF THE PROGRESSIVE MUSICAL ENTERPRISE

As the demand for vaudeville-style performances grew, Lowery, whose name was becoming a household word in the show arena, was in position to capitalize on this demand. He conceptualized a contracting and management organization that would train, develop, and produce talent packages for sideshow and vaudeville presentations. Once prepared, the groups would then be contracted out to the various client circuses and traveling shows that sought this type of entertainment. The operation would manage several shows that would run simultaneously or at different times during a season. As Lowery's operation began to grow, a longer lead time was needed to find the quality of performer he sought. He was intolerant of pretenders but would encourage and even teach honest, willing-to-learn applicants. Lowery guarded his company's reputation and would not allow it to be confused with the tinkers, or less professional groups.

Lowery may have operated under a type of divided structure as early as 1900. Covering Lowery and Green's Improved Minstrels, the press indicated that the group was doing well attributed this success to Lowery's "shrewd careful management." Furthermore, the article reported that "the Eastern show or the big white tent vaudeville attraction will be headed and managed by P. G. Lowery while the western combination is headed and under the sole management of Harry L. Gilliam."[11] The paper offered little further commentary concerning the divided shows, however.

Because of an unidentified illness, Lowery did not tour during the 1902–3 winter season. Instead he stayed in Reece and, according to the

Freeman, was engaged to direct the town's twenty-piece band. He also gave private lessons to four members of his company who accompanied him there: Lee, Morton, Arthur L. Prince, and H. Qualli Clark. Lowery also likely used the time to finalize his new business design.[12]

The formal title P. G. Lowery's Progressive Musical Enterprise first appeared in the May 16, 1903, edition of the *Freeman*. The Enterprise consisted of two complete vaudeville companies, a no. 1 company of twenty-five entertainers under Lowery's direct management, and a fifteen-member no. 2 company managed by Clark. The Enterprise was projected to become a major source of employment for performers of color. The no. 2 company traveled with an outfit bearing the grandiloquent name of The Luella Forepaugh–Fish Wild West Show, a popular small Wild West railroad show.[13]

In addition to Clark, a cornetist, Lowery's no. 2 company included Sallie Lee, Essie Williams, John "Pap" Adams, Steve Adams, Al Hutt, William Johnson, and Robert Brown, George A. Williams, Leah Sanderson, and Daisy Lee. From Iowa, Fred Morton, the *Freeman* agent with this show, wrote to the paper that "we are doing banner business." Like many other shows of the time, townsfolk learned of the Fish show's arrival through a street parade that closely resembled a circus parade. The Fish show featured a steam calliope, reputedly the first new one ever built specifically for a Wild West show. The Fish company's shows and parades received great reviews on its swing through Wisconsin: in Beloit, people followed the parade to the show grounds, anxious to see the free sideshow that kept the audience occupied until the main tent opened, and an Ashland newspaper reported that

The parade of the Wild West Show this morning was first class. It was over three miles in length, and everything advertised, appeared in the procession, including the Sioux, Ogalala Sioux, and other Indians, Mexicans, Cossacks, cowboys, and so on, and Bud Horn, king of the calliope players dispensed music from the calliope. The original bucking elephant was a part of the parade, but he was peaceable as far as could be observed. The livestock made a good appearance and there were some very fine horses in the show. The den of wild animals is something not always seen in a wild west show, and there are other features, some of which are in the two side shows, for instance the looping of the loop by a lady bicyclist, which are not often seen. The company certainly puts up a fine parade, one of the best ever seen in this city, and the show itself is well worth the money.

A record-breaking crowd saw the show this afternoon and the performance was first-class.[14]

The Luella Forepaugh-Fish Wild West show seemed to offer all things desirable in such a production and to have the right formula for a long-running season.

Lowery's no. 1 company also prospered into August 1903. Company members included Harry and Oma Crosby; Samuel Elliott and John W. Carson, percussion; William May, tuba; Pearl Moppins, trombone; James Hall, baritone euphonium; and George McDade, "the Boy Wonder of Knoxville, Tennessee." The *Freeman*'s reports on the show indicated some personnel changes had occurred, not an unusual development as people moved about from one show to another. Charles and Sadie Bruce joined the show at Michigan City, Indiana, while Pap Campbell closed there to join Mahara's Minstrels. Aaron Brown, a bass singer, joined at Petoskey, Illinois.[15]

McDade, whose duties included conducting the company orchestra, drew particular attention from the *Freeman*: "Master George McDade age 13, the youngest orchestra leader and cornet soloist the world has ever known, . . . commenced the study of music at age ten. The cornet was the first instrument, his advancement was so rapid he then took up the study of the violin and today he stands among the best leaders in the profession regardless of his age. Beside his wonderful accomplishment on the two instruments, he possesses the most remarkable ear so accurate and true he can at any time tell the exact tone made on any instrument. He is justly honored the wonder of the 19th century."[16]

Sometime between May and July, the Luella Forepaugh-Fish Show, and with it Lowery's no. 2 show, ran into trouble. On July 30, 1903, the *Janesville (Wisconsin) Recorder and Times* reported that George and Luella Fish had sworn out writs of attachment for protection of their interests. According to this article, Luella Fish had discovered that some of her employees were diverting customers away from the ticket wagons directly to the entry doors, where other conspirators would collect admission fees and pocket the money. Future performances were canceled. The Fishes apparently arranged to have many employees paid off out of the Janesville gate receipts, but those who were less fortunate had no choice but to remain in town until the show could be disposed of. These stranded entertainers continued to offer diversions to the citizens of Janesville:

> While a number of those who had necessary funds have left the city there is still a motley crowd of Indians, Cossacks, Arabians, musicians and roustabouts still here waiting for the money due them from the show people.
>
> Last evening three of the cowboys gave an exhibition on South River Street between Milwaukee and Dodge where a large crowd had gathered. The cowboys rode bucking ponies and made no end of amusement for the spectators. One of the cowboys was thrown violently to the ground, but was not injured and getting up successfully mounted and rode the same pony and was loudly cheered.
>
> The large crowd interfered to a great extent with the exhibition. A collection was taken up among the crowd and about fifty dollars collected.[17]

The show's assets were subsequently auctioned off to the highest bidders. This inventory included "130 horses, wagons, harnesses, show wagons, wild animals, including the elephant, a camel, lions, snakes and other animals, cages, trucks, canvas or tenting, poles, lights, seats, four railway cars, a steam calliope and a large lot of circus paraphernalia." An Erie, Pennsylvania, printer and lithographer, F. J. Walker, bought the entire show for $12,510, approximately the amount of his claim against the show. Walker hired John A. Barton, a former owner of the show, as operations officer and engaged Harry Semon as the show's manager. Walker retained all of the performers who had remained in Janesville and called some others back. The show then returned to the performance circuit. However, it apparently did so without the Lowery Enterprise's no. 2 sideshow troupe, since the *Freeman* reported in mid-August that several performers had been engaged in other activities.[18]

Enterprise no. 1 continued to do good business and at the end of October was in extreme southern Texas, heading northeast. The performers were looking forward to the winter season, when most of them were booked to tour with Lowery and the Nashville Students Company. Lowery had his choice of performers and boasted a roster that included some of the country's best-known performers and entertainers. The *Indianapolis Freeman* reported that those who would be touring with Lowery during the coming winter season included Sam Lucas, whom many people considered "the Dean of the Colored Theatrical Profession." Among the others Lowery had engaged were "Miss Pearl Crawford as Prima Donna, [and] . . . the Crosbys (Harry and Oma) who have the entire season been with the circus. Mr. Crosby, having been stage director the entire season will be a strong attraction, introducing a new set from the pen of one of the best play writers in this country. Mr. Crosby will be Mr. Lowery's principal comedian, and upon him will be the weight of all the comedy through the entire play." On the distaff side, "The bunch of charming soubrettes that will add to the beauty and attractiveness of the show for song and dance and feminine grace and beauty will be the following well known and popular ladies: Mrs. Oma Crosby, Mrs. Emma Foster, Misses Sallie Lee, Essie Williams and Jesse Thomas. Another cause for excitement was the prospect that the company would travel in its own first-class "palace" railroad car.[19]

The Forepaugh Circus closed its season in Cape Girardeau, Missouri, on November 7, leaving company members whom Lowery had engaged for the winter with just two weeks to prepare to go out with the Students' show. Lowery, his promoters, and his advance people immediately involved themselves in the preliminary business of the winter tour. Lowery and his managers and backers, Al and Joseph Baker, went almost immediately to St. Louis to oversee arrangements there, while other administrators Carl Hathaway and R. M. Harvey went to Chicago.[20]

The performers spent their brief hiatus in various ways. The Crosbys vacationed in Cincinnati. Sallie Lee and Essie Williams closed with Sells and Downs, which they had joined after the demise of the Luella Forepaugh-Fish Wild West Show, and were making their way toward St. Louis, as was Lucas. McDade was preparing new cornet and violin solos. And Crawford reportedly refused three lucrative offers to travel overseas in favor of being associated with the Lowery Show.[21]

LOWERY'S 1903 WORLD'S FAIR REVIEW

Despite all of the demands necessary for an orderly but short turnaround time between circus season and road tour, Lowery took on a unique task. In November he visited the 1903 World's Fair in St. Louis and wrote a review of the event for the *Freeman*. This article records Lowery's impressions of a local band performing at the fair and offers a glimpse of his ideas regarding the evolution of African-American bands and orchestras.

For the past few years, I have made a careful study of our musicians and their rapid progress. We find in some localities musical organization[s] that even the most cultured listener is forced to give heed. We are rapidly leaving the rude shores of random work and landing on the cultured shores of musical accomplishments. Even the old self-made system of loud, noisy playing is becoming a thing of the past, but tone culture, perfect attract, the closest attentions that is paid to the principle[s] of music, is fast bringing our colored bands and orchestras on a level with our best white bands; and to exemplify my statement, I will place for your criticism the famous World's Fair Band of St. Louis, a musical organization that stands second to none in the city.

As a colored local organization I am perfectly safe in stating [that] they are in a class by themselves. While spending my vacations in St. Louis I had the pleasure of listening to their different programs from ragtime to opera, and I always left satisfied with no criticisms. Besides their ability as musicians, I found all sociable and unusually friendly, and above all, attentive to their business while on duty, and always kept one eye on their music and one on their leader. I can safely say the World's Fair Band is an organization without five or six leaders, but a body of fine gentlemen I can recommend to the profession.[22]

These performers could not have received a better boost to their careers than Lowery's praise in the *Freeman*.

Harry and Oma Crosby, who had been performing with Lowery, also appeared at the fair, where "they did their work well, being the only colored specialty people on the pike, where there were performers of every race that inhabits the globe". None are more popular at this great show than this clever little soubrette, and this eccentric comedian.[23]

THE TWENTIETH-CENTURY NASHVILLE STUDENTS

The 1903 edition of the Nashville Students opened its long-running season in Mascoutah, Illinois, on November 16. The company reportedly was in great form and performed to a standing-room-only audience that saw several strong attractions, including Lowery, Crawford, the Crosbys, and Lucas. According to the *Freeman*, "Sam Lucas, stage manager, deserves special credit for his careful arrangement of the show. It is universally admitted that Mr. Lucas' reputation as a high-class actor and comedian is unquestioned. He is justly termed, as billed with the show, 'The Prince of All Actors.'" The show also included Lee, Williams, William May, James Hall, Pearl Moppins, John Jones, Gambretta Garrett, Tom May, Mr. and Mrs. S. B. Foster, and George McDade.[24]

By December 1903, the Lowery troupe had completed its tour of Kentucky and was headed into Illinois. The members described their trek as successful and were delighted with their new railroad car, which they named *Pana*. The *Freeman*'s correspondent reported,

The company numbers twenty-two members. . . . Sam Lucas, our active stage manager, has always a keen eye and a sharp ear, and is always perfecting the show. . . . Miss Pearl Crawford easily catches the audience with her charming voice; her songs are as cheerfully applauded in America as when she was abroad in spite of the prejudice that predominated in this country. The Crosbys are a great benefactor to the show, always catching their audiences. Miss Essie Williams and Sallie Lee come in for equal shares of the entire performances. Their professional style never fails to call for encores. The Fosters are active members in the company; they cleverly represent themselves all through the performances. The well-known Ike McBeard is with us, taking the comedy role of the show. Credit is due his efforts, Master George McDade, the boy wonder, is without doubt the coming rival of P. G. Lowery. Mr. Lowery wishes to state publicly he has the field yet without a struggle. His tones are brighter, [and] clear[er] than ever. His peculiar dash and vigor always catches his audiences. . . . Sam Elliott, our chorus director, has greatly improved the singing with the show.[25]

The Christmas season of 1903 found the Lowery Company traveling still in Illinois and Missouri. Mr. and Mrs. George Orrendoff treated the entire group to a grand reception in Atlanta, Illinois, and the performers spent December 20 in St. Louis. McDade assumed the responsibilities of orchestra leader after S. B. Foster closed to take a position in Chicago.[26]

In early 1904, the *Herald* announced that Lowery and his troupe were returning to perform in Eureka: "While the company bills, 'Not a Minstrel Show,' the piece is in reality a musical extravaganza of noisy comicality set to light music containing more than ordinary merit. The music has lots of 'go' in it, more of it than in most of the new Musical Comedies now before the public that are very successful. . . . The musical numbers are of the latest and sang as only the colored people are capable of singing them, taken in all the company is a good one, and up-to-date."[27] With their new show format, the Students were primed to present a blockbuster performance at Eureka's opera house.

Arriving in Eureka, "the Nashville Students were awfully surprised . . . at the massive crowds to welcome Mr. Lowery home. Cheers rang up, after which the [Eureka?] Concert Band of thirty pieces struck up a lively march while the Nashville Students were ushered into cabs and were led to the opera house, which was completely sold out before the company reached the little city. The largest audience ever known to gather in the opera house greeted the show that night."[28]

THE ENTERPRISE CONTINUES

P. G. Lowery's Progressive Musical Enterprise was operating nonstop. Lowery's ads in the trade papers began to tout even more heavily the promise of year-round work, a significant enticement to performers who disliked the prospect of job hunting after each season. Since many performers tended to remain with the show, personnel turnover was decreasing. The short breaks between seasons offered time for rehearsals, planning, and finding new personnel. Then the Enterprise moved out again.

Apparently, Lowery's Progressive Musical Enterprise continued in a management role, preparing and packaging shows under contract for several touring companies in addition to keeping his main show in operation. Periodically, he would run ads in the *Freeman* for musicians to appear in shows which apparently were not his no. 1 (Lowery) show, as he would simultaneously be involved with other aspects of his Enterprise.[29]

Lowery opened the 1904 circus season with Forepaugh and Sells Brothers on April 18 in Philadelphia. Lowery had added Henry McDade, a trombonist and the brother of Little George McDade, and the famous Carter Trio—Lewis, Mim, and Mack. In addition, the roster included Lowery as bandmaster; George McDade as orchestra leader; Tom May on cornet; Pearl Moppins on trombone; J. L. Jones and Robert Grant on alto horns; George Hill on clarinet; Sam Elliott, who played percussion and doubled as the stage manager; and Johnnie Carson, percussions. The singers were Arthur Wilmore, Arthur Wollige, the Carter Trio, Emma Thompson, and Sallie Lee.

Although the demands of the traveling performance troupe were rigorous, there was occasionally some time to relax, when other companies would put on special performances to entertain the Lowery group. Billy Kersand's Minstrels entertained Lowery's company in St. Louis, en route to Philadelphia. Whitney and Barnard of Dale's Troubadours entertained the Enterprise in the course of their stay in Philadelphia during the opening of the 4-Paw Season. When Lowery's group played Albany, New York, the performers were entertained by Diggs and Ridley. In Boston, Lowery's company had at least three social outings, and Arthur Wollige married Elizabeth Evans. Socialization with other troupes and individuals provided a means of refreshment as the Enterprise rolled on.[30]

After Boston and a series of one-night stands en route, the 4-Paw made its way north. During May and early June fierce storms hampered some performances, but by late June, the show had clicked and the weather was cooperative. The troupe wound up its stand in New England and moved into Canada, where the show continued to develop and improve. According to the *Freeman*, "The chorus work is well harmonized this season.... The vaudeville part of this company is easily the best singing company of its kind in America." The paper also reported that the band and orchestra were also improved over the previous season, as all the performers played with the tone quality and swift execution that Lowery required and that always caught audiences' attention.[31]

In mid-November, the Enterprise was on the verge of closing its triumphant season with Forepaugh and Sells. Most of the company had remained throughout the season, although clarinetist Hill had departed as a result of illness. From the point of view of both Lowery and of his performers, it had been a good season: "we are about to close a record breaker; not missing but one performance; having no wrecks and but little sickness." Unfortunately, after those words were written, misfortune befell the company. During a performance in Tarboro, North Carolina, on the closing day of the season, November 19, the show was robbed. Circuses had previously been considered "safe" places, and robberies were most unusual. For the reason, Lowery might have reconsidered his position there. On the other hand, due to the fact that he had so many professional connections, he might simply have taken a better job for himself.[32]

After the tour closed, some of the performers went home, while others joined other companies. The Carter Trio planned to stop off in St. Louis on its way home to Paris, Texas; Thompson joined a vaudeville company; Lee went first to St. Louis and then home to Columbus, Ohio; and George and Henry McDade returned home to Knoxville, Tennessee. The McDade brothers had previously announced plans to study in Boston if they were not in Lowery's employ.[33]

THE PITTSBURGH PROJECT

At the end of the 1904 circus season, Lowery made a connection with Professor W. A. Kelly, the director and leader of Kelly's Famous Band and Orchestra, a popular fixture in Pittsburgh. Lowery went to Pittsburgh to direct this thirty-piece band and to assist Kelly in teaching at his music studio. In December, shortly after his arrival, Lowery informed the *Freeman* that he would not publish the musicians' names until "the band has arrived at a satisfactory point." By February 1905, however, Lowery apparently felt that the band had developed to a point that he could publicly discuss the band's personnel and performance schedule.

Pittsburgh, Pa. has a right to be proud of her new concert band organization under the direction of P. G. Lowery, band master, and Fred Hammonds, business manager. This organization is composed of thirty-five musicians, the pick of Allegheny County. Each department of the band is represented by men that have had years of experience. Among those we may mention are Al Robinson, first violinist and leader of Prof. Kelly's famous orchestra; Wm. Lee, ex clarionetist of the Old Kentucky Company's band; Prof. W. A. Kelly, B. Gilmore, Fred Williams and Al Harris, all clarinet players of recognized merit. The cornet section is headed by L. E. Gamble, who has experience, practice, and ability. Fred Hammonds, the saxophone player, is in a class to himself. The band gives its first concert February 27 in Turner's Hall, Pittsburgh, Pa.

This concert was quite successful, attracting an audience estimated at one thousand people. The concert featured a saxophone solo by Bessie Davis and of course a cornet solo by Lowery. The *Freeman* praised the performance, reporting that it received "rounds of applause." The group presented a second concert at Turner's Hall on April 6.[34]

In all likelihood, under Lowery's guidance the group changed its name from Kelly's Band to the Commercial Band of Pittsburgh. The program from Theodore Roosevelt's 1905 inaugural parade shows that the musicians marched with the Commercial Club of Pittsburgh.[35]

While working with Kelly, Lowery was also involved with Frank Mahara, a minstrel show producer. In November 1904, Mahara had announced his hiring of Lowery as bandmaster of Frank Mahara's Minstrels beginning on August 1, 1905. In February 1905, the *Freeman* reported that Mahara had arranged to have Lowery direct Mahara's "big band of 40 pieces, which Mr. Mahara will place before the public early next season. It will be comprised of the best colored musicians in America." Although Lowery personally was spending the 1904–5 winter season in Pittsburgh, Mahara may have engaged the Enterprise to provide a cadre of entertainers for his winter show. The *news*paper also disclosed that Mahara had signed Lowery "for a long period." However, Lowery appeared with the Mahara show only during February 1905. The terms of the contract may have permitted Lowery to commute back and forth between Pittsburgh and wherever Mahara's Minstrels were performing. The *Freeman* reported on April 8 that Lowery had "opened a studio of music at 1200 Franklin Street, Pittsburgh, Pa."[36]

Lowery continued to hustle in his usual fashion, keeping a current project—or projects—in hand while planning his upcoming activities. P. G. Lowery's Progressive Musical Enterprise was becoming big business, providing employment for numerous entertainers. On April 1, the *Freeman* carried Lowery's advertisement for eight women, fifteen musicians and four comedians for a "big R.[ail] R.[oad] Carnival Company."[37]

THE GREAT WALLACE SHOW TOUR

Lowery joined the Great Wallace Circus on April 19, 1905, and the Enterprise opened with the Show on April 29 in Peru, Indiana. During its first month, the show moved through Ohio, West Virginia, and Pennsylvania. Lowery's company was the first troupe of color to travel with the Wallace Show. It was said that Lowery's troupe was also the best financially supported attraction on the road at that time. The band and orchestra consisted of William May, tuba; Thomas May, cornet; James Hall, baritone euphonium; Samuel Elliott and John Carson, percussions; Fred C. Richardson, clarinet; J. Anatole Victor, violin and orchestra leader; and J. W. Mobley and William Jones, trombone. Harry and Oma Crosby were again with the tour, with Harry singing and serving as stage manager. The other soubrettes were sisters Sallie and Daisy Lee. Arthur Wallace (Wollige) was also a singer. Mr. L. Norman provided the comedy, and J. Edward Hunn was also with the troupe.[38]

By June the group was settling in and a few personnel changes were taking place. Mobley closed with the show in Braddock, Pennsylvania, and was replaced by Henry Washington from the Pittsburgh Commercial Band. Norman and Hunn also left to join other shows, and Whitney Viney joined the show.

"Wanted at Once" advertisements appeared in the *Freeman* on July 15 as Lowery searched for "good bass singers." He even offered to advance a train ticket. A suitable response was not long in coming. The next "Notes from the Enterprise" indicated that "Tony Bearfield, a basso with a phenomenal voice from East St. Louis has joined us and has added greatly to the show. Besides doing chorus work, he renders a solo which pleases." The same report also contained the unfortunate news that Elliott had left the show as a result of his ongoing illness. Overall, Lowery stated that he was very pleased with the Great Wallace Show and his vaudeville company: "good people, good treatment and great show."[39]

In late July, J. D. Howard, correspondent for the *Freeman*, visited the show in Rushville, Indiana. Accompanying Howard on that visit was Elwood Knox, the paper's owner. Howard found

everybody smiling and evidently prosperous. P. G. Lowery's Progressive Musical Enterprise is the banner feature of the Side Show this season. The company is certainly making good. Mr. W. H. McFarland, the genial manager . . . emphasized in a later statement that negotiations were on between Mr. Lowery, Mr. Al Martin and himself to take the Lowery aggregation South after the close of the present circus season with a tented exhibition devoted to the highest expression of vaudeville and minstrel art.

The show is produced on a large elevated stage with the orchestra arranged in the rear. Each performance averages about forty-five minutes, and six are given during the day and night.[40]

Mid-August found the company in good spirits in their fourteenth week of travel. The weather was agreeable and everyone was physically well. One small misadventure was reported almost as an afterthought: "Our car was badly smashed while being transferred. It happened that all had gone to dinner. Had we been on the platform some one would have been hurt or killed."[41]

No such incidents marred the month of September, when the Enterprise swung back into Indiana, although Daisy Lee became ill and Arthur L. Prince opened with the show. The talk of the show was that Lowery was about to take over the Nashville Students in collaboration with Al Martin and Ben McFarland of the Great Wallace Show, a splendid idea that would be welcomed by the show-loving public. By October, the tour was winding down, and the performers were making plans for their well-earned period of rest and recuperation, with Lowery intending to spend a few weeks in Columbus, Ohio. The circus closed its season on October 24 in Williamson, West Virginia.[42]

Details regarding the following winter season are scarce. Lowery worked with an obscure show called the Watermelon Trust Minstrels in December.

At the close of the season, George McDade went to spend the rest of the winter with his parents in Knoxville, Tennessee. Lowery returned to Pittsburgh. Sometime during this busy season, Lowery composed what Charles Bennett Jr. termed the "most famous circus tune . . . the extremely difficult 'Prince of Decorah Gallop.' . . . This is one of the most difficult of all circus tunes to play . . . and has been used by many circus bands." Still available commercially, the composition has an extremely fast tempo and is highly syncopated, or ragged, requiring extensive technical and physical skills.[43]

By May 1906, the Enterprise was again running at full speed. As the *Freeman* put it, "P. G. Lowery's Progressive Musical Enterprise is back under the white tent again with the same old bunch and a few good additions." The nineteen performers who headed west included Thomas May, George Thomas, Fred C. Richardson, Anatole Victor, T. H. Lewis, Henry Washington, William Jones, James Hall, William May, John Carson, Whitten Viney, Arthur Wollige, Sallie Lee, Harry and Oma Crosby, Bessie Higgins, and Sis Wiggins. George and Mamie Thomas joined the troupe at Muncie, Indiana. The band was well rehearsed, and the singers engaged their audiences. At the end of May or beginning of June, however, the company received the unfortunate news that former Lowery musician Henry McDade, on his way home to visit his ailing father, had fallen under a train and been killed.[44]

June 1906 ended for the company with the news that the Forepaugh–Sells Brothers Circus was now the property of the Ringling Brothers. In 1905, James A. Bailey had gained full ownership of the Forepaugh–Sells Show but almost immediately sold half of its interest to the Ringlings. A year later, the Ringlings owned the entire show. July found the Enterprise rolling into Iowa. A combination of midsummer heat and personnel attrition began to exact its toll on the company. Sallie Lee and Oma Crosby became ill, and then the Crosbys closed with the show, as did George and Mamie Thomas and T. H. Lewis. Billy Arnte, the "Carolina Sunbeam," subsequently replaced Harry Crosby.[45]

As the summer heat and many miles passed, the company continued to deliver great entertainment. Lowery had arranged a whole new program.

At Oskaloosa, Iowa, C. L. Barnhouse Publishing Company executives gave Lowery a new trombone duet that was "cleverly executed" by William Jones and Henry Washington. Arnte caught the audience with his buck-and-wing dancing and singing, and Sallie Lee recuperated and brought down the house with her singing.[46]

The Great Wallace Circus season was originally scheduled to close during October, but the *Freeman* announced that the Enterprise would continue en route until November 5, weather permitting. Lowery "celebrated his birthday on the cars, October 11, with a highball party." The newspaper also reported that the Nashville Students unit of the Musical Enterprise would open in Peru, Indiana, on November 16. With the end of the circus season, Lowery's lieutenants busied themselves preparing for the Students' tour season. John Carson was in Indianapolis engaging talent, and James Hall and later Sallie Lee passed through Indianapolis on their way to Peru. The break between seasons would last about one week.[47]

"NOT A MINSTREL SHOW"

"This is not a minstrel show," declared the lead line in the *Freeman*'s review of the 1906 Nashville Students' show, "but a musical entertainment full of comedy and high-class specialties."

The first part represents the colored race in its rude state, just after their free-dom. This part is ably handled by Billy Arnte, representing Ben Sigh [Bensiah] Williams, the father of a talented family, seeking a musical education. In this old man character, Mr. Arnte is in a class by himself. Mr. Whitten Viney as a rich cotton dealer, interested in the education of the colored race, adds greatly to the reality of the play by handling his part well. Miss Lee does herself great credit as Henrietta, a natural-voiced singer, daughter of Ben Sigh Williams, and Paul Carter, the Southern Star comedian, keeps the house in a continual roar of laughter by the way he so ably handles Toby's part (mischievous boy), supported by a company of singers and dancers, producing a novelty first part that catches the public.

The second act, or olio, is a high-class vaudeville, featuring P. G. Lowery, cornet soloist; Billy Arnte, the monologue king; Thomas and Thomas. Miss Sallie N. Lee, possessing a sweet voice and pleasing manner, catches the

high-class theater goers. Rowland the Wonder is without doubt the best tramp juggler in the business. Arnte and Carter leave them all laughing, both being comedians, singers and dancers. The crowning feature of this part is the Cathedral Choir,
arranged by our stage manager, George Thomas, consisting of fifteen of the best
voices in the show.

The third part represents our race after having the advantages of schooling.
In this act, Miss Lee ably displays her ability as an actress, and George Thomas as
manager of students. Rowland as the butler, Whitten Viney as the female cook
and Paul Carter as a supposed prince of Africa. All have a share in the success of
the play, Tony Barefield, in his original African costume, with the lion voice,
completes the bill, making a show that pleases everybody.[48]

This dramatic production represented the culmination of the turn away
from minstrelsy. Such dramas were becoming the accepted bill of fare for
the better touring companies on the road.

"Business is good," announced the *Freeman*, singling out Viney and
Carter for particular accolades. Lowery's twenty-piece band was larger
than his previous units, Arnte was a box office hit, and Lee had become the
show's prima donna, receiving "a banquet on her birthday, November 26.
After the bountiful refreshments were served, the company surprised Miss
Lee by presenting her with appropriate presents from each member of the
company. This event is one long to be remembered."[49]

Again the show continued to prosper despite personnel changes.
Rowland, the juggler, closed with the show to go into vaudeville, and the
Stevens Sisters' singing, dancing, and talking act was added to the roster.
The show became more polished, and its reception grew accordingly as it
toured the eastern and southeastern United States at the end of 1906 and
beginning of 1907. Lowery's band was cited for proving that musicians of
color could play classical music with technical proficiency and musicality:
"Mr. Lowery reports the best band of his career, judging from a musical
standpoint, and we notice Mr. Lowery still holds fast to the oar of honor
as the greatest cornet soloist in the United States, and with his usual untiring ambition, is pulling up the stream of success."[50]

During the 1907 season, the *Freeman* referred to the group as
"C. H. Sweeney's Nashville Students," working "in mighty unison with

P. G. Lowery's Concert Band."[51] This phrasing suggests some sort of arrangement under which Lowery furnished talent packaged as a complete show and Sweeney provided the operating capital and retained management of certain aspects of the show. Profits would be divided among the principals. Lowery was unquestionably capable of serving as the show's manager, and in practice, he did so. But some professional doors were more readily opened by whites than by blacks, creating the need for working "in mighty unison," for mutual benefit.

As had now become his standard practice, Lowery was simultaneously looking forward to the upcoming circus season, when he would take his show into what was now called the Hagenbeck-Wallace Circus. The *Freeman* carried his ads for talent, and arrangements were being made for the usual smooth transition.

THE CARL HAGENBECK-GREAT WALLACE COMBINED SHOWS

The 1907 season began not with the Great Wallace Circus but instead with an amalgamation called the Carl Hagenbeck-Wallace Circus. In many locales, Lowery's arrival with this show became a major event. Lowery's "reputation in Pittsburgh, Pa. as a bandmaster, music teacher, and a gentleman has made him the pet of the flock, which fact was plainly demonstrated in his last visit to the city with the Wallace and Hagenbeck Combined Circus." When the show arrived in Pittsburgh, the Iron City Lodge of the Colored Benevolent Protective Order of Elks of the World feted the performers with a lavish welcome banquet that included speeches and the presentation of "costly gifts" to Lowery.[52]

The tour with Hagenbeck-Wallace was for the most part of standard Lowery quality. The company did good business and attracted large, appreciative audiences. In early August, the *Freeman* published its annual review of the show, observing that although the sideshow was not the main attraction of the circus, Lowery's act would attract the attention of the most casual observer.

On entering the sideshow, which is the Mecca for those that love fashionable vaudeville, you will first see Prof. P. G. Lowery and his concert band. This band will impress the visitor very much on account of its not equaling the average "colored" band—that is, they render music like Creatore's band. Prof. Lowery has full control of his men, and every time he waves his baton, it is not a sound of harshness that you hear; it is simply melody, because Lowery has learned his men what reading and melody are, and that no man must fake in his organization.

That Lowery and his band will draw lovers of good music was a self-evident fact. . . . Lowery manages to get astonishing effects from his instrumentalists. They owe their conception to his vivid imagination, and their execution to a marvelously well-drilled number of bandsmen. His staccato chords come upon one with the startling suddenness of an electric shock. They make one jump with their unexpectedness; they are like the crack of a Mauser rifle, when playing grand opera. Let them play you a rag, and you cannot help but dance and feel happy, because they have a lovely swing to their playing.[53]

The review also cited sideshow manager Ben McFarland for his style of management, which was unlike that of the old-fashioned "circus boss." McFarland, who was white, was complimented for his manner with the blacks he supervised and with those who patronized the show. He was perceived as "the first showman to give the Negro a chance—that is, to make good for himself, if he would try. There was everywhere evidence of this fact, because you saw Negroes doing something for a salary in every department [of the sideshow]. Mr. McFarland has been rightly dubbed the 'Abe Lincoln' of the show business."[54]

This 1907 company carried nearly all of the same names as the preceding season: Whitten Viney, Billy Arnte, Billy May, Arthur Wollege, Tony Barefield, Mamie and George Thomas, John Carson, and Paul Carter. Anatole Victor at first traveled with the group but fell ill at Plymouth, Indiana, and closed at Indianapolis. Henry Washington succeeded Victor as orchestra director. James H. Lewis joined the show at Mt. Carmel, Illinois, and Mose Harris joined in East St. Louis, Illinois. Leading lady Sallie Lee closed in July, going to New York for the remainder of the summer, and was replaced by a woman named McClelland.[55]

The Hagenbeck-Wallace Circus season closed at Roanoke, Virginia in mid-November. Performers set off in different directions to rest and to prepare for the coming season with the Nashville Students or some other group. Arnte closed with Lowery and became the stage manager for Marshall's Old Plantation Show. Lowery spent some time in Indianapolis with Elwood Knox and then went home to Kansas for a rest, visiting his mother, hunting, and riding horses on his family's farm.[56]

Lowery also devised one additional project for the good of all entertainers and show people. The *Freeman* reported that following Lowery's leadership, the foremost black show managers, including James Wolfscales of the Cole Brothers Vaudeville and J. E. "Pap" Adams of the Great Norse and Rowe's Vaudeville Annex, had come together to form a "combination"—a rudimentary labor organization. The group's stated objectives included the protection of "our people by demanding first-class accommodations and keeping the salaries up to standard." The organization also pledged to protect itself and its management groups by not hiring anyone who was under contract to another show or who had been fired from another show for negative behavior. The same issue of the newspaper also announced that Lowery would be serving as director of Pittsburgh's concert band and carried an advertisement for the position of secretary to Lowery.[57]

During the 1907 winter season Lowery again headquartered in Pittsburgh, where he conducted bands. On February 23, 1908, he conducted the First Regiment of the Knights of Pythias Band. Reviews indicated that Lowery had again developed a very fine band, and the performance was outstanding.[58]

Lowery heard rumors that during the coming season the Buffalo Bill Wild West Show and Barnum and Bailey would be waging territorial circus warfare against the Hagenbeck-Wallace Show. The battleground would probably be the state of Indiana. In retaliation, Hagenbeck-Wallace would start its 1908 season earlier to establish a solid foothold before the other two shows hit the road. In addition to his work with the Pittsburgh bands, Lowery now began to get ready for the impending spring circus season. The Enterprise would begin rehearsals on April 27 at Peru, Indiana, with an opening date of May 2. Thus, the performers had only five days to make the transition from minstrel/vaudeville format to circus sideshow.[59]

Observers eagerly anticipated Lowery's new show, which reportedly would have the largest company ever under canvas. Lowery was quoted as saying that the band would be better than any former band. Various big-name entertainers were spotted passing through Indianapolis on their way to Peru to join Lowery's company: Ome Mason, Charles and Blanche Beechum, Fred and Hattie Garland, Slim Mason, John Carson, and a recuperated Anatole Victor. In addition to these performers and Lowery, the troupe also included Henry L. Rawles, Tony Barefield, J. R. Johnson, Billy May, Tom May, Johnnie Carson, Georgie Hill, Bill Jones, W. Bolden, John "Junk" Edwards, Estella Phillips, and James Hall. Some of the new performers represented significant personnel changes. Fred Garland was the new trombone soloist, and his wife, Hattie, replaced Sallie Lee as the leading lady. Junk Edwards and Charles Beechum took Paul Carter and Billy Arnte's places as comedians.[60] As the show moved back to the east after playing as far west as Denver, the players began to eagerly anticipate their three-week stand in Chicago. The band personnel had changed somewhat during that western leg of the tour, and the power of the troupe apparently had increased. Lowery's band now consisted of "Tom May and William Bolden, Cornets; George Hill, Clarinet; H. L. Rawles and Anatole Victor, Altos [horns]; Fred Garland and William Jones, Trombone; James Hall, Baritone; Billie May and Tony Barefield, Bass; Johnnie Carson and Jack Johnson, Drums." The *Freeman* also noted that the band had five soloists in addition to Lowery himself "every once in a while." The Hagenbeck-Wallace Show closed in the vicinity of Paxton, Illinois, in early October, returning to winter quarters in Peru to rest, recuperate, and retool for the next season, which would start about ten days later.[61]

The 1908 Nashville Students opened at Vicksburg, Michigan, on October 10 to a standing-room-only audience. Lowery had teamed up with Fred A. Morgan and his wife for this season's production. Their comfortable railroad car had been refurbished inside and out, and the food was good. These items alone portended a good season.[62]

The show format was the same, not a minstrel show but a kind of vaudeville–pageant combination. This season's company included Henry Jefferson; Elvis Mason; Tony Barefield, bass soloist; James Hall; H. S. Rawles;

Charles Beechum, stage manager and comedian; William May; Tom May; William Jones; F. C. Smith; Charles Milton; Ed Hendricks; Frank Slayton; Fred Garland; Anatole Victor, orchestra leader and alto horn; William Baldwin (Bolden?); Blanche Beechum, leading lady; Eva Prince, who performed a hoop-rolling act; Florence Hall, singer and soubrette; Callie Vassar; Eva Nolan; Cordia Cunningham; Nellie Frost; Goldie Morlan; and Hattie Garland. Johnnie Edwards played Bensiah Williams in the tableau, and Jack Johnson portrayed the master of the plantation. Another female singer, Carrie Gilbert, also joined the show.[63]

The Garlands' part of the tour was short-lived this season, as Hattie became ill at Marquette, Michigan, and they left the show there around October 24. At Lansing, Michigan, Cora Spires, a baritone soloist, joined the company. November 1908 found the troupe still playing in Michigan. Victor had written a new rag, which was well received by the audience, and singers Gilbert and Vassar drew ovations. In late November, the company learned of the death of a former member, Mamie Thomas. Victor subsequently closed with the company to freelance in Michigan and was replaced by W. A. Kelly, Lowery's friend and colleague from Pittsburgh.[64]

In December the company moved into Missouri, Kansas, and Illinois, including a performance in Eureka. The company members looked forward to visiting Lowery's farm to sample some home cooking. Florence Hall became ill but remained with the show, and the Garlands rejoined the troupe at Shelbyville, Illinois. Fred Richardson, a clarinetist, joined the show at Collinsville, Illinois.[65]

During the beginning of 1909, Lowery began his customary preparations for the coming circus season with the Hagenbeck-Wallace Show. The 1908–9 Nashville Students had been a hit, perhaps more than any other version of the show, and Lowery was pleased.[66]

According to the *Freeman*, the 1909 Hagenbeck-Wallace Show had "so many features to recommend . . . to the public that it is almost a puzzle for one to find out just where to commence. It requires two big sections of the trains for the transportation of the outfit. The management seems to have omitted nothing that belongs to a well-regulated circus." The writer noted the presence of people of color in "every possible place they could be used." Providing Hagenbeck-Wallace with a priceless public relations boost in black communities nationwide, the *Freeman* stated, "This is a strong inducement for the colored patronage to this show wherever it may appear. The big show is headed through the Virginias and *The Freeman* takes special pride in recommending it to the race throughout its course in the Southland."[67]

The newspaper projected that the circus's "most pleasing" feature would be Lowery, his concert band, and his minstrels in the sideshow, again crediting Lowery with the best talent in the business—an "Opera House under canvas." The roster of performers read very much like that of the 1908–9 Nashville Students Company, although a new comedian, Billy Earthquake, joined Enterprise veterans John Edwards, Charles Beechum, and Harry Crosby and served as the new stage manager. Lowery also tried something new in the business: a female interlocutor, Blanche Beechum, whom the *Freeman* described as "finished and pleasing. . . . She sidesteps those tiresome drags that one is forced to stand for oftentimes in colored minstrel shows."[68]

The show's two other female performers were Johnella Gay, in her first appearance with Lowery, and Essie Williams, who had rejoined his company after performing with other troupes. Lowery's band consisted of fourteen pieces, one of the largest sideshow bands on the circuit, and included Lowery; Arthur Jackson, clarinet; Tom May and Tom Tolliver, cornets; Anatole Victor and H. L. Rawles, alto horns; James Hall, baritone; Irwin Brown and Arthur Hill, trombones; William May and Tony Barefield, basses; and John L. Edwards, Charles Beechum, and Blanche Beechum, drums. From this group also came the orchestra under the direction of Victor, who had rejoined Lowery's Enterprise this season.[69]

Moving to the northwest, the circus arrived in Seattle, Washington, on July 4. There, Lowery's company witnessed a performance by the Dixie Land Minstrel Company, with a thirty-two-piece concert band conducted by James Lacey. The two groups clearly admired each other professionally, and Lacey "did everything in [his] power to make us perfectly welcome by placing the entire company in the reserve seats in their large theater to witness the best show of its kind ever before the public."[70]

The Hagenbeck-Wallace Circus moved on to Portland, Oregon, where the Lowery troupe was met and greeted by "a group of *Freeman* readers" who apparently were quite influential in the community: "This being Lowery's first visit to Portland many new acquaintances were formed. The leading citizens and business men took an active role in welcoming P. G. Lowery's . . . company to Portland." The entire company was taken to the Golden West Hotel, where the performers were accommodated with all expenses paid. A number of the hosts were members of the local Elks' lodge, and they chartered transportation to take the entire company to an Elks' picnic for further entertainment.[71]

The company continued to put on strong performances, and "Lowery's Minstrels" were the "talk of the West." As usual, some personnel changes occurred: Harry Crosby and Johnella Gay closed at Salt Lake City, where Robert Giles joined the troupe, and Jennie Gallie later joined the company in California. Also considered noteworthy was the arrival and receipt of a new set of Leedy drums for Charles Beechum and Johnny Edwards.[72]

Moving eastward, the train brought the troupe into Missouri and Kansas during September. Victor found time to marry Mary Washington in Indianapolis. Fred C. Richardson, a clarinetist who had previously worked extensively with Lowery, joined the show in St. Louis. Lowery stopped over in Kansas City to make arrangements for the upcoming winter show season, and he celebrated his fortieth birthday, October 11, in Texarkana, Texas. The group performed in Arkansas, Oklahoma, and Louisiana during October with the same roster with which it had returned from the West. Billy Earthquake planned to go into vaudeville after November 8, but the remainder of the company apparently intended to go on the winter tour with Lowery and Morgan's Minstrels. The Hagenbeck-Wallace Circus closed at Dyersburg, Tennessee, on November 6.[73]

A RETURN TO MINSTRELSY

The company opened the 1909 winter season in December under the name Lowery and Morgan's Mighty Minstrels. The program was a hybrid of aspects of minstrelsy and vaudeville. According to Lowery and Morgan, this troupe had been formed a year earlier from a group of performers "left over" from the Hagenbeck and Wallace Shows. The opening "minstrel first part was a scream from opening to closing." The second part was less like minstrelsy and more closely akin to a rewrite of the dramatic musical production style presented by the 1906 Nashville Students.[74]

The 1909 show included many of the same people who had traveled with Lowery's Hagenbeck-Wallace Circus show during the previous season as well as some newcomers, including Charles and Blanche Beechum; Ben Johnson; Logan Kitchen; Junk Edwards; Elvis Mason; Milton Guthrie; Fred and Hattie Garland; Essie Williams; Tony Barefield; Jennie Gallie; Callie Vassar; Carrie Gilbert; William May; Thomas May; Richard Gardner; Arthur Hill; Anatole Victor and his wife, Mary, a singer; and H. L. Rawles.[75]

In March, at the end of another successful season, Lowery and Morgan's Minstrels came to Indianapolis, where some businesses declared a special holiday so that their employees could attend the parade and show.

P. G. Lowery got his men into line at 10:50 A.M. Everybody stopped in the midst of their daily toil to listen to that great band led by Prof. Lowery. At the head of the parade was Mr. Elwood C. Knox, accompanied by one of the representatives of the management, in a decorated carriage. A halt was made at *The Freeman* Office, where a band concert was given which was enjoyed by over a thousand people.

The parade of the minstrels was to the city what Barnum & Bailey's parade is to the largest city in the west. Everybody turned out despite the cloudy, cold weather.[76]

The show was also well received. The *Freeman* indicated that the expected clean performance of minstrelsy was indeed delivered.

Messers Lowery and Anatole Victor opened up the performance with a telling cleverness of musical talent in operatic tones. The talent of Mr. Victor as a leading violinist, was at once established, and the audience did not refuse to give him and his selection of musicians a great amount of applause. What struck the sightseer forcibly was the way in which the company went through their opening chorus in a very "stagy" manner. Junk Edwards, Slim Mason, Logan Kitchen and Charles Beechum handled the end seats in a very creditable way.

Mr. Lowery proved himself to be, as he is said to be, by the press, "the world's wonder" as an extraordinary classical soloist on cornet. He received the hand clapping of over five hundred thorough critics of music. We were glad to see Miss Carrie Gilbert make her debut as a top-notch comedienne of high marked ability. Her costumes and her singing . . . were worth the price of admission. She is pretty and delightful in her every move.

What put life into the performance was the well-written sketch of "Jack Johnson's Return," by Logan Kitchen and Slim Mason. This is an afterpiece that will make good in any theater before any audience in the country.

The sketch . . . has to do with two tramps going to a small town and passing themselves off as Jack Johnson the prizefighter and Bill DeLaney the trainer. DeLaney entices Johnson to [a] saloon where there is a possibility of getting something to eat, but they fail. However they wind up in a sporting lodging house, . . . and are given every courtesy. When they are in the height of their glory, a clever boxer appears, who challenges champion Johnson. Where the real fun comes is in the fight that Slim Mason and Junk Edwards take part in. You could not help but laugh at the funny antics in which both men get in because of their builds. Junk Edwards is short with short arms, and Slim Mason in long with a lengthy reach. . . . These two comedians are truly bound to be successful in the stage world. Mr. Mason is a clever actor and has the making of a great playwright.

The newspaper concluded that Lowery's organizational skills and especially his musicianship were "serenely great."[77]

After this gala performance, the performers turned their focus and energy to resting a bit and to preparing for the circus season, which was only about four weeks away. Jennie Gallie closed with the show to join the Sells-Floto Circus. Charles and Blanche Beechum also left to join Terry's Big Company. Slim Mason went to Louisville, Kentucky, to visit his mother, and from there joined the Sells-Floto Show. Walter Reid, a trap drummer from the Royal Theater, signed on with Lowery for the circus season. Lowery spent a few days in Wichita, Kansas, and then went to visit his stepmother. Rumor had it that he even rested a bit.[78]

The season opened on April 23 when the Hagenbeck-Wallace Circus began a week of performances in Peru, Indiana, as a kind of dress rehearsal to affirm that all was ready for the road. Lowery again had developed a good company. The band and show had some familiar names: Lowery, director; Anatole Victor, alto horn, violin, and orchestra leader; William Bolden, cornet; William Jones, trombone; James Hall, baritone; William May and Tony Barefield, bass; Junk Edwards, bass drum and comedian; and soubrette, Essie Williams. Many new performers had also joined: Walter Lee, clarinet; Frank Miller, trombone; Walter Reed, snare drum; Walter Thoman, W. A. Bruce, and George Day, comedians; and Hazel Kinney, Emma Foster, and Julia Thomas, soubrettes. Another new attraction was South Sea Island Joe and his wife, Bena, who amazed the audiences with demonstrations of rare native weapons and curios.[79] Singers James and Mamie Brown apparently joined the show, en-route, about mid-June.[80]

Lowery's group had an unusual number of new faces this season because of the revival of the Forepaugh–Sells Brothers Circus after a hiatus of at least two years. Although the Ringling-owned Forepaugh operation and Hagenbeck-Wallace were competitors, P. G. Lowery's Progressive Musical Enterprise was the contractor responsible for the training, development, and production of the sideshows for both circuses. On May 10, the two shows met in western Pennsylvania, where Forepaugh was performing in McKeesport and Hagenbeck-Wallace was playing in nearby Homestead. (It was not unusual for two competing circuses to have scheduled concurrent performances only a few miles from each other.) Early that morning, "Lowery, Tony Barefield and Wm. May came to McKeesport, PA, to get a look at the largest, best show on the road. . . . Before either show started their parade, the Forepaugh–Sells side show band and minstrels took great pleasure in showing Prof. P. G. Lowery . . . our fine palace car." In the evening, after the Forepaugh Show had ended, Lowery alumni Tom May, Logan Kitchen, and H. L. Rawles visited their former colleagues on the Hagenbeck show. The time was spent renewing old friendships, meeting new people, and enjoying being together.[81]

The rest of the season was generally uneventful for Lowery's company. In Mason City, Iowa, twelve male performers and supporting staff members were honored by being initiated into the Knights of Pythias, a popular order with those in show business. In addition to admission ticket sales, the company apparently generated money by selling photos of the performers and by selling songbooks containing simplified arrangements and/or the lyrics to the tunes performed in the show.[82]

The show closed its season on October 24, 1910, at Trenton, Tennessee. Anatole Victor took on work as the orchestra leader at the Crown Garden Theater in Indianapolis. Lowery, Gilbert, James and Florence Hall, and brothers Thomas and Billy May went to Columbus, Ohio. Although some units of the Enterprise may have done so, Lowery did not personally perform on a 1910 winter tour. Instead, he operated his now well-known Progressive Musical Enterprise from Columbus. It is likely that some of the other shows on the road that season were managed by the Lowery organization.[83]

THE COLUMBUS CONNECTION

Rather than sitting idly while he "rested," Lowery involved himself with different areas of musicianship and business. The *Freeman* reported that by January 1911, Lowery was making arrangements for three different attractions for the summer season—his own traveling show plus two more engaged groups. In addition, he traveled between Columbus and Leavenworth, Kansas, to make arrangements for the April 10 opening of the Great Parker Shows, another of his contracted clients.[84]

In early 1911, the *Freeman* reported that Charles Beechum would join Lowery during the upcoming season with Hagenbeck-Wallace; shortly thereafter, the newspaper announced that Fred C. Richardson was under contract. By March, the *Freeman* printed an avalanche of reports proclaiming names of Lowery's performers, even before Lowery himself could make the announcements. Veteran Thomas May would serve as Lowery's assistant, and other old hands included Tom Tolliver, Tony Barefield, James and Mamie Brown, and Anatole Victor. New additions mentioned were Paul Halyard, Alex Valentine, Elk Venable, and Ben Lee.[85]

The Enterprise was growing along with the demand for black entertainment. The *Freeman* proudly announced,

Since the close of the season 1910 we find six circuses are advertising for colored bands and minstrels that have never carried a colored company before. Much of the success and advancement is due to the untiring efforts of the managers in charge of the different companies in securing first-class talent and to better their companies each year. And with the support of such men as Prof. Wolfscale, H. Q. Clark, S. T. Dunsmore, R. Roy Pope, J. E. Adams, Will Reid, Bismark Ferris, Thomas May, H. L. Rawles, B. F. Reynolds, and others, P. G. has a perfect right to feel proud of the circus vaudeville and minstrelsy.[86]

Of the ten managers/directors listed, six were Lowery products.

Although Lowery was not the first band director of color to perform with a circus, he was credited with creating the sideshow entertainment combination of bands and minstrels in vaudeville performances. Before 1899, when he introduced this type of show using twenty-three musicians and performers at New York's Madison Square Garden while traveling with Forepaugh and Sells Brothers, a circus band of ten pieces had been considered sufficient.

In March, Mr. and Mrs. Walter Coleman hosted a luncheon in recognition of Lowery's influence on Columbus's musical climate during his visit. Approximately a week later, Lowery and the musicians who had traveled with him for ten years of record—Thomas and Billy May and James Hall—were treated to a festive dinner, an "enormous gathering of all the leading musical organizations and musicians of Columbus, O. To show appreciation of [Lowery's] presence in the past five months." Lowery used the occasion to publicly pay homage to Sol P. White, conductor of the Ninth Ohio National Guard Band, who had paved the way for Lowery's accomplishments in the circus world.[87]

About this time, the *Freeman* began to speculate on the personnel of the season's various Lowery shows, carefully observing the movements of the performers. Logan Kitchen passed through Indianapolis en route to Pennsylvania to connect with H. L. Rawles, who was preparing a production for Howe's Great London Shows. Anatole Victor traveled through Indianapolis on his way to Peru, where he would meet with Lowery. Speculation turned into outright pronouncements.

Thomas May, cornet soloist, will be P. G. Lowery's assistant this season. His brother, William May, will also be at his old post with the aggregation.

The St. Louis party that will join P. G. Lowery's big vaudeville company and band are Miss Webster, Tom Tolliver, Fred Richardson, and the old reliable T. Barefield.

Paul Habyard, Alex Valentine, Elk Venable and Ben Lee are all new editions [sic] to P. G. Lowery's Progressive Musical Enterprise with the Hagenbeck-Wallace Shows this season.

Indianapolis will be represented by such talented people as Chas. Beechum, Mr. & Mrs. James Brown, and Prof. A. Victor with the P. G. Lowery concert band with the Hagenbeck-Wallace Shows this season.

Subsequent reports indicated that Lowery was in Kansas City and Leavenworth, Kansas, placing the finishing touches on an Enterprise production for the Great Parker Show.[88] Thus, Lowery's hiatus in Columbus resulted in three shows on the road during the 1911 circus season.

The Enterprise's annex unit with the Great Parker Show opened in Leavenworth, Kansas, on April 10, 1911. The *Freeman*'s correspondent reported,

The show carries twenty-five people, band and orchestra. The roster consists of the following: R. Johnson, manager; J. L. Davis, band leader; Carl Travis, assistant leader; Wm. Lee, orchestra leader; Doc Ford, stage manager; W. A. Bruce, assistant stage manager; J. Davis, cornet; C. Davis, cornet; W. A. Wallace, trombone; Doc Ford, alto; Wm. Lee, alto; R. F. Martin, baritone; C. B. Miller, clarinet; Harry Murray, snare drum; W. A. Bruce, bass drum; J. Wallace, tuba; Doc Ford and W. A. Bruce, extreme ends; R. F. Martin and Carl Travis, second ends; R. L. Jones and W. A. Smith, third ends; Blanche Beechum, interlocutor; Jennie Gallie, soubrette; Etta Walker, soubrette; Eva B. Prince, soubrette; Sig J. Arcaris and wife, impalement act; J. E. Edwards, mimic; Condonna, musical act; Madame Zouza, snake charmer. Our car "Dixie" is the swellest car carried on the road for colored performers under canvas.[89]

Rawles served as band director and manager for Howe's Great London Circus Annex, which opened in Verona, Pennsylvania, on April 15. The troupe opened with a full band that included Rawles on baritone euphonium, Al White and H. T. Howard on clarinet; Ed Tolliver on alto horn; A. N. Parker on violin and alto horn; Max Shaw and Irving Brown on trombone; E. P. Wood on bass; J. L. Holmes and Logan H. Kitchen on

Ad for P. T. Wright's Nashville Students Colored Comedy Company, 1998–99. The company was highly selective and the ads included pointed statements to the untalented: "Amatuers [sic] Save Stamps."

The open-call ad was notice to all in the profession that a company was being formed or restaffed for a coming season. In this February 12, 1910 advertisement from the *Freeman*, Lowery identified the quality of performer that he sought by unhesitatingly admonishing applicants to play it straight with him.

"Wanted Quick" or "At Once" ads were urgent pleas for immediate help. Though musical and theatrical preparedness were still required, these openings were perhaps the best opportunity for a novice trying to break into the business.

Photographs and figures courtesy of the author unless otherwise noted

"Little" George McDade, the Boy Wonder of Knoxville, Tennessee, was a protégé of P. G. Lowery and leader of the P. G. Lowery Orchestra. A child prodigy, McDade reportedly had perfect pitch and excelled both as a virtuoso cornetist and as a violinist. Photo courtesy of Mrs. George McDade.

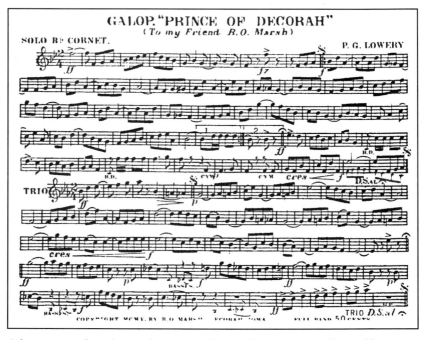

Solo cornet/conductor's score for Lowery's "Prince of Decorah Galop." Termed by some musicians as the most famous circus tune, this fiendishly difficult composition is highly syncopated and meant to be played at an extremely fast tempo. Still available commercially, "Prince of Decorah Galop" is not for the average band, the semiprofessional performer, or the faint of heart.

Lowery & Morgan's Minstrels bill poster, *Freeman*, March 12, 1910. On the Monday that this show was advertised to occur, businessmen in Indianapolis announced a special holiday so that employees could attend the parade and show. Larger lithographed versions of this same ad were posted throughout the area.

LOWERY & MORGAN'S
MINSTRELS!
TOMLINSON HALL!
ONE NIGHT ONLY
Monday, March 14.
25 FUNNY COLORED PEOPLE **25**

Big Band and Orchestra

The following well known Stars are included: The Beechums, The Garlands, Junk Edwards, Miss Carrie Gilbert and Prof. Antone Victor's Celebrated Orchestra—Featuring the Undisputed World's Greatest Cornetist,

Prof. P. G. Lowery
and his Grand Challenge Band.

Watch for the Grand Street Parade!
At 10:00 a. m.,
On Indiana Ave., Senate Ave. and West Street.

ADMISSION: BOXES AND FIRST FLOOR, 50C; BALCONY, 25C

Grand Ball After Show. Tickets on Sale at Freeman Office.

WANTED ---------------------------------- WANTED

For the Great J. H. Boyer's
Fashion Plate Minstrels
A $75,000 Production
2 ---------- BIG SHOWS ---------- 2

Three of the finest Pullman palace cars with each show,
Two of the best equipped tent theaters,
wardrobe the finest, furnished by the company, no ladies in parade

Eighteen comedians, 16 Soubrettes, 4 novelty acts, 8 tenor singers, 8 bass singers, 10 drum majors, 35 first-class musicians for each band, preference given to those who double stage. Can feature two lady soloists, cornet or trombone. State your lowest salary and what you do and will do in first letter. Do not misrepresent yourself; no time to dicker. Show opens in April. Boozers, disorganizers, and would-be show managers. don't answer this ad. Address all mail to:

P. G. Lowery
Care J. H. Boyer
918A St. Clair Avenue   East St. Louis, Illinoisi

This talent wanted ad, printed in the *Freeman* on March 12, 1910, and again on January 27, 1912, touted the extravagant performances of Lowery & Boyer's Minstrels. Stories were circulated that Lowery would hire a hundred performers and travel overseas.

As Lowery's fame spread, others tried to capitalize on his name and reputation. In this *Freeman* ad Arthur L. Prince, who once worked with Lowery on the Fashion Plate Minstrels, made a less-than-subtle attempt to profit from this association by claiming that he could teach one to play like Lowery.

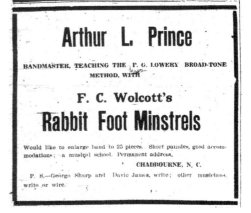

Arthur L. Prince
BANDMASTER, TEACHING THE P. G. LOWERY BROAD-TONE METHOD, WITH

F. C. Wolcott's
Rabbit Foot Minstrels

Would like to enlarge band to 25 pieces. Short parades, good accommodations; a musical school. Permanent address,

CHADBOURNE, N. C.

P. S.—George Sharp and Davie James, write; other musicians write or wire.

Lowery's 1916 Sideshow Band with the Hagenbeck-Wallace Circus. Front row (l to r): William Hoy, percussions; Mrs. Elmer Payne, soubrette; Mrs. Carrie Lowery, soubrette; Mrs. Charles Creath, soubrette; and Jackie Smith, bass drummer. Middle row (l to r): Elmer Payne, clarinet; Maylon Hall, clarinet; Thomas May, cornet; Perry G. Lowery, cornet and director; Charles Creath, cornet; William Moore; and Irving Richardson (possibly in reverse order). Back row (l to r): William May, tuba; Lafayette Williams, trombone; John Eubanks, baritone euphonium; and Ed Carr and Tony Barefield, tuba.

Solo B flat cornet part, "Pee Gee's Blues" © 1919. This composition was written by one of the best "Colored" composers of the era, H. Qualli Clark of Pace & Handy Music Company, New York. For a time Lowery was Clark's employer and cornet teacher.

P. G. Lowery's Band with Ringling Brothers, Barnum & Bailey Circus (ca. 1922). Photo courtesy of Circus World Museum.

With this 1922 letter Lowery hired William "Shorty" Matthews, a working relationship that would last through the late 1930s. Matthews, a much sought-after woodwind player and perhaps one of Lowery's favorite musicians, kept an anecdotal diary that described the itinerant lifestyle typical of musicians of that era, recorded the movements of the Lowery organization with the Ringling Brothers Circus, and encapsulated Lowery's professional endeavors in Cleveland. Courtesy of Circus World Museum.

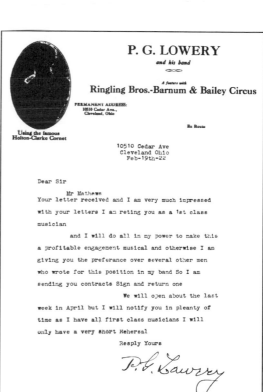

P. G. Lowery's Side Show Band & Minstrels, 1930. William "Shorty" Matthews is seated front row, right end.

Lowery (standing fourth from left) with the Cole Brothers Circus Sideshow Band, ca. 1935. Photo courtesy of Circus World Museum.

Lowery (standing far right) with the Robbins Brothers Circus Sideshow Band, 1938. Photo courtesy of Circus World Museum.

P. G. Lowery's Band and Minstrels with the Downie Brothers Circus, 1939 (Lowery standing center). The Downie show, unlike the other Lowery-affiliated shows, which traveled by rail, was a "motor show" that traveled the roads in a convoy of trucks. This show was perceived by some as a downward professional step for Lowery.

Lowery (standing center) finished his career with the 1942 Cole Brothers Circus Side Show, pictured here.

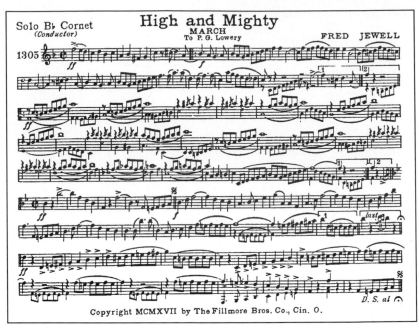

"High and Mighty," written by Fred Jewell, © 1917, was dedicated to P. G. Lowery.

Jacob M. W. Watkins (left) and the author at the grave site of Perry and Carrie Lowery, Harvard Grove Cemetery, Cleveland, Ohio, 1999. The burial place is doubled, with Carrie's body buried atop the coffin of Perry.

Perry George Lowery, Cole Brothers Circus, 1940. This photograph is unique in that it portrays the "World's Greatest Colored Cornet Soloist" with a trumpet and not a cornet.

percussions; T. M. Thomas on B-flat cornet; and L. H. Gilbert, assistant bandleader, on E-flat cornet. According to Rawles, the band and minstrel were making good, both on parade and in the annex.[90]

The third Enterprise unit traveled under Lowery's personal supervision and was again associated with the Great Hagenbeck-Wallace Show, which opened in Peru, Indiana, on April 20. In addition to Lowery, serving in his customary positions as cornet soloist and bandleader, the musicians included A. R. Hoffman, sideshow manager; Thomas May, cornet; Tom Tolliver, violin and cornet; Fred Richardson and James Brown, clarinets; Anatole Victor, alto horn and orchestra leader; Ben Lee, alto horn; Elk Venable and Alex Valentine, trombones; Paul Halyard, baritone; William May and Tony Barefield, basses; Junk Edwards and Edward Neville, percussions; and Paul Halyard, violin. Veteran singer Essie Williams continued Lowery's practice of using a female interlocutor. Other women in the troupe were Winona Criegler and Mamie Brown, singers and soubrettes. Junk Edwards and Charles Beechum were the comedians. James Brown also sang. Finally, South Sea Island Joe and his wife, Bena, also performed.[91]

At several stops on the tour, Lowery and his troupe were honored by local groups, and Lowery's company in turn would entertain other traveling shows when their paths crossed. Lowery was also honored when Chicago's Frank Holton Company gave him a new cornet, "one of our very best highly engraved gold cornets in an elegant plush-lined case, as a present and token of our appreciation to you for your untiring efforts to show the world that Frank Holton & Co. makes the best band instruments in the world." In June, Lowery's mentor, George Bailey, visited the troupe: "He made parade and filled in the entire day. The entire band joined in making his visit an enjoyable one." Along with these happy occasions came the occasional sad events. On November 11, the *Freeman* brought the sad news that W. A. Bruce, who closed with the show on June 2, had died.[92]

After the season ended in late November, Lowery spent some time visiting the *Freeman* offices in Indianapolis. The newspaper reported Lowery's pride in having had the season's largest band and minstrel company and in the fact that several performers had been with him for as long as twelve years. Lowery's brother, James, who along with another brother, Jesse, was a supporting partner in the Progressive Musical Enterprise, met P. G. in Indianapolis to transact business relating to the show. James brought a two-thousand-dollar railroad car, which he presented to his brother, who then left for Nashville, where he would prepare for the winter season.[93]

TO HIM WHO HUSTLES

In 1910, the popularity of the vaudeville-type show was continuing to escalate. Producers converted or modified their shows to accommodate the demand, and the terms *vaudeville* and *minstrelsy* became practically interchangeable. Describing vaudeville's progress, Bernard Sobel observed that

The incipient American variety show . . . took root here and acquired a certain flair and polish during the mid-nineteenth century. . . . The assorted acts, or specialties, remained basically the same in character but increased in number and quality by borrowing liberally from the varied forms of native American variety entertainment, as exemplified in minstrel or medicine show, circus, concert, dime museum, town hall entertainment, beer hall or honky-tonk, even . . . from the legitimate stage, concert hall, grand opera, ballet, musical comedy and pantomime.

As Carolina Caffin put it, vaudeville "offered a gorgeous variety of brands: from melody extracted from the unwilling material of xylophones and musical glasses through the varying offerings of singers and instrumentalists, both comic and serious, to the performers of high-class chamber music or the singing of an opera diva."[1]

John E. DiMeglio remarked that vaudeville was the "most popular form of entertainment in a period of American history when many significant changes were taking place through the nation."[2] The shows provided many opportunities for performers, especially African-Americans, to display their many talents and capabilities.

Like P. G. Lowery, some of the best entertainers gained recognition by performing in the circus during the summer season and touring with minstrel shows or on the vaudeville theater circuit during the winter season. Trouping was their livelihood, and they respected it. The best performers continuously strove to develop and sharpen their craft. Joe Laurie commented on the personal quality of the "vaude" act in small theaters, where the audience was nearly onstage with the performers, and noted that "Negro performers did more than just singing and dancing; they contributed their many talents to all lines of vaude. . . . Florence Hines was a male impersonator; the Great Gowongo, a magician, Allie Brown, a slack-wire walker (I don't know of another one who did this work). Wilbur Sweatman, a great clarinetist, played vaude for years. The Negro contributed plenty of color to vaude in more ways than one."[3]

Lowery, a quiet innovator, made three important business decisions that contributed to his continued success both as a performer and as an entrepreneur. First, he skillfully revised his production format to meet the tastes of his audiences, and he developed his capability for show presentations in several markets simultaneously. Even as he geared up Lowery and Morgan's Minstrels for the winter 1912 season, talk around the circuit held that Lowery had something "up his sleeve"—and some people speculated that he had something up both sleeves.[4]

Second, Lowery formed a coalition with prominent individuals in the profession, a syndicate that included J. H. Boyer of East St. Louis, Illinois; Fred Morgan, "the best railroad contractor in the business, [who could] handle and railroad a show from a two-horse show to the Barnum and Bailey, and never get tied up"; and Lowery's brother, James.[5] This team provided capital and business connections that nearly guaranteed the venture's success. These names would become well known in the workings of Lowery's Enterprise.

Morgan's managerial expertise was indispensable so that a show could move around without the sort of logistical problems that could spell economic catastrophe. Boyer, a millionaire promoter, had access, a valuable commodity in the business. His financial acumen and know-how could get Lowery into places that might otherwise have been almost completely off-limits. In January 1912, the *Indianapolis Freeman* published the big news that Boyer would be sending Lowery "and a concert band of forty picked musicians to Europe in 1913." Musicians interested in overseas travel should contact Lowery at once.[6]

Lowery's third critical strategy was to continue to hone his skills as a performer and as a person, dominating the entertainment field as an individual attraction. Furthermore, despite his success, Lowery maintained his connection to the people, thereby contributing to his ongoing popularity. Despite his fame and acclaim, Lowery appeared to be more interested in making a way for other professionals than in promoting himself.

LOWERY AND MORGAN'S MIGHTY MINSTRELS, 1911–1912

Lowery and Morgan's Mighty Minstrels opened the winter season at Mendon, Michigan, in December 1911. The *Freeman* reported that

large audiences have been the rule and the public seems assured that the unexpected offering is of double worth of attractiveness. . . . Mr. Arthur L. Prince is [the] stage manager of this happy bunch, and the public critics are well aware of the fact that there is nothing left undone. The first part runs like clockwork. In fact it is something out of the ordinary as a novelty opening for a minstrel show. The skyscraping tenors balance the attractiveness of the female voices, thus adding charm to the well-trained chorus. Too much can not be said of the olio and afterpiece, as far as a pleasing performance is concerned. The band and orchestra are both well balanced.[7]

On Christmas Day, the performers inaugurated the Majestic Theater in Nashville, Tennessee, with two sold-out shows. Although the theater was still under construction, a situation that created some production problems, the Nashville audience was certainly interested in patronizing the show, even though the house wasn't "equipped and ready to play a first-class company." Furthermore, "inclement weather the remainder of the week caused a slight decrease in business."[8]

During the show's tenth week out, in early February 1912, business remained good. The Lowery and Morgan company was in Missouri, and the colder temperatures did not adversely affect the audiences. The show was now booked through September 25, and Lowery planned to take the show under canvas around April 15. Some observers thought that the show was just lucky, but Lowery and Morgan's success resulted from reputable quality performances, not chance. The show's flashy parades, good band, tasteful entertainment, and careful management epitomized the qualities sought out by the public.[9]

This was not a small-time operation: from its inception, it had the resources to go and grow simultaneously. In early February, the *Freeman* indicated that "Robert Martin, the peerless baritone, and Logan Kitchen, a droll comedian, joined in Jefferson City, Missouri. The band at present numbers eighteen. New faces are coming on every week, and by February 25 the company will have an enrollment of sixty-five people." Some of the performers traveling with the Lowery and Morgan Show were being groomed and rehearsed for J. H. Boyer's Fashion Plate Minstrels, which would open in March. And in another stroke of managerial wisdom, whenever performers closed or were beset by illness or other adversity, replacements were available at barely a moment's notice. And by mid-February, Lowery had received three hundred letters in response to the January call for performers who wanted to travel to Europe.[10]

Lowery emphasized the quality of onstage presentations and performances, using strong, innovative stage managers who functioned as both executive officers and artistic directors. Those persons who remained with the Enterprise seemed to be the ones who readily grasped Lowery's philosophical concepts of production. For example, the *Freeman* noted that "Prince believes in running a minstrel just like clockwork, and moreover, he demonstrates the cleverness of comedians, singers and dancers by the addition of finishing touches."[11]

Lowery veterans Junk Edwards, the Beechums, and Carrie Gilbert continued to wow the audiences, but Lowery, never one to rest on his laurels, continued to seek out new talent. According to the *Freeman*, rumors had it that Lowery was "negotiating for the Martin brothers, baritone and trombone players, formerly with the Mazeppa's Famous Show Band. . . . These two youngsters [also] have a very neat acrobatic act."[12]

Things were going well, and morale was high. One writer even composed a poem about the troupe:

> *The Fashion Plate minstrels are still in line*
> *The band and orchestra they say'll be fine*
> *Singers and dancers won't be slow—*
> *For Arthur L. Prince will stage the show.*
> *Bright as the sun shines in the west,*
> *J. H. Boyer's will be the best*
> *As sure as the roses in the merry spring blooms,*
> *Mr. Hart, of Chicago, will make the costumes.*
> *Like the ripples follow the waves to the sea,*
> *So will prosperity follow thee.*
> *If from me you'll take this tip:*
> *Get with the Fashion Plate's lucky trip.*[13]

March found the Lowery and Morgan troupe in Iowa, continuing to perform before consistently crowded houses. In addition, local fans continued to fete the company members at private gatherings. In mid-March, the *Freeman* published a review of the show:

The theatrical entertainment is on at once after a short overture. Whoever selected the performers, all of whom are colored, knew what they were doing. They give a snappy show, every performer being a star.

The show is minstrel in effect. U. S. Thompson (Slow Kid) is on one end and Charles Beechum . . . is on the other end.

P. G.'s band played all the while, thus adding to the gaiety of the nation. The members of the band are: P. G. Lowery, cornet; Anatole Victor, violinist; Billie May, tuba; Tom May, cornet; William Lee, drums; J. H. Tobias, trombone; Max Shaw, trombone; Elmer Payne, Clarinet.[14]

Sobering news began to intrude, however. First, the players learned that Beno, who had appeared with her husband, South Sea Island Joe, in the Hagenbeck-Wallace sideshow, had died on February 5. Then came the information that P. G. Lowery's brother and business partner, James, had died of pneumonia in St. Joseph, Missouri. P. G. escorted his brother's body back to Reece, Kansas, for burial. The Mighty Minstrels' personnel offered their condolences—and their assurances about the show's continued prosperity—to P. G. via the *Freeman:* "Owing to the death of our friend J. H. Lowery, better known as Uncle Jim, we have been absent for a few days from our beloved band leader, P. G. Lowery. We as a company want to extend our heartfelt sympathy to him and the rest of his family. The show is getting along fine, doing good business everywhere."[15]

Shortly after rejoining Lowery and Morgan's Minstrels, P. G. again departed to join the Hagenbeck-Wallace Circus for the season. In his absence, Fred Garland became director of the Lowery and Morgan band. Despite the upheavals caused by all of these changes, the impending marriage of performers Hattie Harden and Roy Burgin kept spirits high. Logan Kitchen would give the bride away, and monologist John Dennis would be the best man. Violinist Paul Halyard was practicing the Mendelssohn's "Wedding March."[16]

THE FASHION PLATE AND THE GREAT WALLACE CIRCUS

March 1912 brought interesting reading in the trade papers. Lowery was advertising for show personnel to work either in the Lowery and Morgan show or in the Great Hagenbeck-Wallace Circus, which would soon open its summer season. On March 16, the *Freeman* printed the call that many performers had anxiously been anticipating: "All performers and Musicians engaged for season 1912–13 with J. H. Boyer's Fashion Plate Minstrels report on private palace car 'Sadowa,' located on terminal track, relay station, East St. Louis, Ill., April 8, 9 A.M. ready for rehearsal, as per your agreement and contract. . . . Can use a few more musicians who double stage or orchestra."[17]

The Fashion Plate Minstrels reopened in May at the Grand Opera House in Alton, Illinois, and

delighted an appreciative audience. . . . The hearers were charmed with the way in which Arthur L. Prince arranged and rehearsed the performers, who set forth their best efforts with songs of our noted composers of almost every country.

The first part setting was elaborate, the scenery being magnificent and the costumes of the best.

Mrs. Mabel Toliver, our prima donna, was perhaps the hit of the first part with her song, "Red Flowers in May," which showed by its rendition the composer's genius. The manner in which she sang gave the true impression of the master's ability to compose as the birds sang in the spring. Each act in the olio received rounds of applause, and some took curtain calls. The afterpiece was also a scream.

The band, under the leadership of Mr. Arthur Prince, showed the composer's efforts to give gentle dignity to the music rendered before the public.[18]

The next significant report on the Fashion Plate appeared in the *Freeman* during August, when the troupe was touring northwestern Canada and just missed a direct hit from a cyclone. Morale remained very high, and the players were looking forward to fulfilling their coast-to-coast bookings that season. A no. 2 Fashion Plate show was scheduled to go on the road around September 15. Moreover, the *Freeman* announced that "the following season the big musical enterprise will employ several competent musicians and organize the first and only colored concert band to make a tour of the world."[19]

After its near miss with the cyclone, the Fashion Plate began comparing itself to weeds that were capable of thriving in any climate. Lowery visited the group during September and was pleased with Prince's work with the show. Carrie Gilbert had introduced a catchy new child imitation act, and several new members had joined and enhanced the show. Boyer was also "pleased with the minstrel show furnished by P. G. Lowery." Fashion Plate performer Ruth Sprague summarized the company's tour experience with a poem:

OUR SEASON
(The Fashion Plate Minstrels)

We hoisted up our white top the fourteenth day of May,
Everyone was cheerful, happy, bright and gay
P. G. Lowery gazed all 'round, and slowly to Prince did say:
"I place this band within your charge, now direct them how to play."
So Arthur L. Prince, with baton grand, took full charge of the minstrel band
Which gave great satisfaction, we're proud to understand.

The merry maids and jesters all wore a pleasant smile, and everyone was lucky to save a snug little pile.

So we all clasp hands and say adieu, for November second our tent season's through.

And may we meet again 'ere late, with three big cheers for the Fashion Plate.

We're glad we had such a pleasant roam, our bags are checked for home sweet home.[20]

While the Fashion Plate conducted its successful tour, Lowery and another company traveled with the Wallace-Hagenbeck Circus. In addition to Lowery, the musicians in this troupe included Arthur Wright, solo cornet; Tom May, first cornet; John Tobias, first trombone; Max Shaw, second trombone; Johnnie Haywood, baritone; Billy May, tuba; Anatole Victor, alto; Elmer Payne, clarinet; Charlie Beechum, snare drum; and Willie Lee, bass drum. U. S. Thompson and Charlie Beechum were the comedians, and Irvin Richardson was a tenor singer. Female performers were Alma Richardson, Lizzie Thompson and Callie Vassar Hill. The *Freeman* printed a review written by an "unknown traveling critic" that proclaimed Lowery's company "excellent":

P. G. Lowery's Progressive Musical Enterprise is the right name for the . . . company. I have had the pleasure of visiting every circus carrying colored companies, and can safely say without fear of contradiction that the company with the Wallace Shows, under the management of P. G. Lowery is far the best aggregation under the white tents. It is an even-balanced company, carrying a band, orchestra, and show. From the first number from the band on parade one can easily detect each member of the band is from the old school. Each member has had personal teaching from Prof. Lowery, and play only as trained musicians. Their [tones] are well sustained with perfect [attacks], which give a great effect, especially for a small band. The old, self-made style of blasting and each member trying to outblow his fellow bandsman is done away with in this organization. The concert work by the band inside of the tent is the most pleasing of any band I have had the chance of listening to, consisting of popular overtures, catchy rags, and heavy marches. One can easily detect the musical ability of such men as A. A. Wright, Thomas May, John Haywood, John H. Tobias, Wm. May and A. Victor, who handle their independent solos in different selections in artistic style . . . .

The minstrel part of the show is very good. They dress neat and tidy, especially the three ladies, Mrs. Alma Richardson, Miss Lizzie Thompson and Miss Callie Vassar. The two funmakers, the end men, Charles Beechum, and U. D. [sic] Thompson, are two busy bees, and there is not one dull moment.

Special mention is due Mr. Irvin Richardson. [This] high tenor, has such a voice as is rarely heard under the sideshow tent. The minstrel part is ably supported by an excellent orchestra, under the leadership of A. Victor, who I hear has been in the employ of P. G. Lowery for seven years.

This is without a doubt, the most pleasant company I ever had an opportunity to visit—just like one big jolly family. On asking Mr. Lowery how he managed to bring about such unanimous harmony, he replied: "Its all in the system—when to speak, what to speak, and how to speak."[21]

Beginning in August, Lowery began to promote the Fashion Plate Minstrels' winter season. The *Freeman* announced that the show would open in the theaters in November, with an enlarged company of thirty that would travel in its own Pullman palace cars. Just prior to the show's opening, Lowery promised that it would be "the swellest that ever happened."

The first performance of the winter season occurred in Carrollton, Missouri, on November 23, 1912. The costumes were obviously expensive, and the sets were quite elaborate. When the curtain rose on the first part, it was immediately apparent to the audience that this was indeed a class show.[22]

The show's performers included Lowery, H. A. Griffith, Harper Morgan, Arthur L. Prince, Arthur A. Wright (stage manager), Whitney Viney (choral director), Tony Barefield, Anatole Victor, Thomas May, William May, Charles Beechum, Horace Eubanks, Jay Bryant, H. Mitchell, Mack Shaw, Eugene "Sheeny" Peterson, Daniel Frazier, Fred Morgan (manager), Wilson Hill, William Smith, Callie Vassar, Mattie E. Glover, Carrie Gilbert, Ethel Kinney, and Ruth Sprague Prince. Most of the players were seasoned Lowery veterans, which the *Freeman* noted, "speaks well for the management." The paper also opined that Lowery had gathered "a choice selection of clever performers for the present season, with gorgeous costumes, magnificent scenery, a well-staged performance and the best minstrel band."[23]

January 1913 found the troupe traveling through Illinois, with everyone in good health and high spirits. As they traveled, the highly creative performers developed more unusual acts. Charles Beechum and Ethel Kinney created a rollicking comedy act, and Arthur Prince became a hoop roller and developed an act featuring his "educated hoops." Soubrette Carrie Gilbert closed the olio section of the show with singing, dancing, and an up-to-date monologue. A prima donna, Vivian DeGloveour (aka Glover) joined the group and pleased audiences with her high-class singing, and Ruth Sprague Prince was also bringing down the house. Male singers Jay Bryant, a "silver-toned" baritone, and Tony Barefield, the basso profundo, scored high marks. The show was booked solidly until the end of March.[24]

Early February found the Fashion Plate performing in Beardstown, Illinois, a return date at which the show broke all previous attendance records, as a result of which the managers were "wearing smiles that won't come off."[25]

Also in February, Lowery's company had an incident involving Greer and Greer, performers who arrived to join the show at Sidell, Illinois. Although the Greers claimed to have sent a telegram announcing their intention to join the show, Lowery had never received their message and thus was not expecting them and had no place for them. It was important to Lowery that the public not perceive his operation as one that would stand up contracted performers, so his integrity was on the line. The Lowery players apparently donated money to pay for tickets so that the Greers could travel to Chicago to find work. But after the duo "had received the collection, also a nice seat at the opera house, and breakfast, dinner, and supper, and the luxuries that we have on the car, they began to brighten up and said they were members of the C.V.B.A. [Colored Vaudevillians Benevolent Association] and could get a ticket and any amount of money they cared for. Naturally, that was a professional shock to the members. Now they regret their sympathy, and the change." Despite the Lowery organization's carefully maintained wholesome image, two grifters had fleeced the show.[26]

Despite this incident, the Fashion Plate Show ran a record twenty weeks and was in excellent fiscal health. All performers were paid every Sunday morning, an event that was significant because in a few weeks the company members would go in various directions with other shows, some of them less financially sound. As the *Freeman* summed up the season, "The show has been a decided success in every respect; the management can boast of a season without one losing week, and the company can boast of good treatment, accommodations and a musical benefit both vocal and instrumental."[27]

As was his practice, Lowery looked ahead to the Wallace-Hagenbeck summer season during his winter tour. Another quick transition would be necessary, since the Fashion Plate was scheduled to close its season in Mascoutah, Illinois, on March 30 and the Wallace Show would open in St. Louis on April 12. During the hiatus, Tom May, A. A. Wright, and J. Bryant prepared to join Lowery on the Hagenbeck-Wallace tour. Carrie Gilbert visited Callie Vassar at her home in St. Louis. Lowery went to St. Louis for a time and then went home to his farm in Reece, Kansas. Then he headed for Peru, Indiana.[28]

UNSETTLED CLIMATE

The rehearsal date for the Hagenbeck-Wallace Show quickly arrived, and Lowery and his troops set about their work. The season's troupe was called the P. G. Lowery Dixie Minstrels with Lowery serving as white top band director and Anatole Victor as orchestra director. The opening performance was to be in St. Louis's Coliseum on April 12, 1913, but on March 26, the circus's winter headquarters at Peru, Indiana, was "literally swallowed by the rising waters. . . . The news was flashed around the globe and then the telegraph wires went dead and it was several days before the thousands of friends throughout the world could allay their suspense by any reliable news as to actual conditions."[29]

Despite the devastating effects of the flood, which included the loss of both human and animal lives, the Hagenbeck-Wallace Show went on. The circus opened in St. Louis as scheduled, having purchased replacement animals and repaired and repainted damaged gear along the route.[30]

Lowery and his crew escaped the raging waters unharmed and appeared on the sideshow as usual. Winton Williams, a writer for the *Freeman*, succinctly summarized the show: "Hagenbeck-Wallace Shows in Indianapolis—The usual parade—P. G. Lowery and his bunch." Lowery's musicians included A. A. Wright, J. Bryant and Thomas May, cornets; Anatole Victor and J. L. Edwards, alto horns; A. J. Johnson, baritone; Billy May and Tony Barefield, tubas; William Hay and Mack Carter, percussions; A. G. Fredericks and Earl Granstaff, trombones; and Horace Eubanks, clarinet. The comedians were U. S. "Slow Kid" Thompson and J. L. Edwards. The female performers were Callie Vassar, Mrs. Hattie Edwards, and Carrie Gilbert, with Tony Barefield, J. Bryant, Mack Carter, and Earl Granstaff the male singers.[31]

Those who saw Lowery's show that summer rated it as excellent. They were apparently taken with its technical proficiency, its professionalism, its artistry, and perhaps its recovery after the flood. Just over two months after that disaster, the *Freeman* published a review of a show in Harrisburg, Pennsylvania:

The Barnum & Bailey show, also the 101 Ranch were in our city with colored companies and bands previous to the engagement of the Wallace & Hagenbeck. But as soon as Lowery's band played their first number, one could see a vast difference in Lowery's band, and the bands with the other companies. After the street parade, I had the pleasure of hearing the musical first part, which was composed of good singing, and new and funny jokes. The full orchestra wields an able part in the minstrel first part. The three ladies all possess good voices and dress as swell as our regular vaudeville stars.

The band renders an excellent program, consisting of overtures, selections, solos, and standard marches. When hearing Lowery's band, one can easily tell they are from the Lowery school. The band was royally received by the musicians of Harrisburg.[32]

The same May issue of the *Freeman* also reported that "the band is making rapid progress. Each member is striving hard to be able to add credit to the world-wide reputation of Mr. Lowery as a bandmaster, and to be able to play with credit in any band in the United States, as P. G. always freely shares his schooling, which he paid very dearly for in Boston." Lowery's band was well balanced and was capable of handling complex classical overtures and other band pieces. Stage manager Wright pressed the company for perfection with his one-word motto, "Improvement." Among the players who received the most positive audience response were William May, Carrie Gilbert, and William Hoy, and the performers' minstrel offerings developed into three distinct shows daily. The opening and closing numbers of the chorus were the highlights of the show.[33]

During the tour, cast members learned that they would have to adjust to changes in management and ownership. A June issue of the *Freeman* reported, "The Hagenbeck-Wallace Show has been bought by the United States Amusement Company. . . . John O. Talbott, formerly of Indianapolis is president of the new company, and Charles E. Cory, of Peru, secretary-treasurer, a nephew of B. F. Wallace, now sole owner of the show, and he and Mr. Talbott will have charge under the new ownership. According to Mr. Talbott, one of the results of change of ownership will probably be the removal of the headquarters of the show from Peru to Indianapolis." This change in ownership did not at first directly affect the performers out on the road.[34]

Lowery began to plan the winter season for the Fashion Plate Minstrels as early as June, when he advertised for three new novelty acts, a chorus director and a producer. The *Freeman* reported that the winter season would open around November 20 and would be "larger than last season, [with a] company of thirty performers and musicians." Another important announcement heralded the fact that Lowery and the Wallace-Hagenbeck Show would be coming to Indianapolis on August 18. The Indianapolis performance received plaudits similar to those that had been accorded to the troupe's earlier shows. The *Freeman* also reported that "all of the work is done without any makeup—the performers wore just their plain faces, and they went big." Lowery's policy of not "blacking up" remained noteworthy. Also in August, Slow Kid Thompson married Letepha Rogers.[35]

But in Bloomington, Indiana, on August 22, the weather again wreaked havoc with the show:

During a terrific wind and rain storm, and just after three thousand people had left the Wallace-Hagenbeck circus on Friday, August 22, the big tent blew down, injuring one show man and causing a loss to the circus of $15,000. . . .

The concert after the afternoon performance had just closed and the crowd had gone, leaving only about fifty employees under the main tent. . . . The heaviest loss was in ruined canvas, about $8,000 worth being twisted and torn until it was practically useless.

When the main tent fell, the center pole thrashed about, tearing much of the canvas into shreds. Animal wagons were overturned, cook tents collapsed and the side shows were blown down. Only two animals were injured, a deer and a llama. . . . Many seats were destroyed and the apparatus in the big tent damaged. Horses were extricated from the canvas and ropes by cutting their harness.

Most of the employees were at supper, but none was injured when the cook tents blew over, although dishes and food were destroyed and many of the showmen lost their evening meal.[36]

None of the members of Lowery's troupe were injured, and the show went on.

But the weather was not yet finished tormenting the Hagenbeck-Wallace Show. According to an October notice, "the deluge of rain that inundated east Texas made it impossible for Hagenbeck & Wallace's Circus to show in Clarksville, Texas. The show jumped to Paris [Texas]."[37]

As the winter season approached, Lowery announced that he had teamed up with J. R. Andrews to manage the show, and Andrews "is sparing neither time nor money to present the highest-class minstrel that has ever been on the road. P. G. Lowery boasts of the best car ever owned by a colored man, and will have the finest accommodations of any car show. . . . The company will number thirty-five people, including two agents." Furthermore, "Lowery's concert band, with his Dixie Fashion Plate Minstrels will number twenty trained musicians." Throughout the remainder of the circus season, announcements regarding the upcoming Fashion Plate tour appeared in the *Freeman*, whetting the appetites of patrons eager to see the group.[38]

In spite of the hardships the company had faced, this was one of Lowery's most successful seasons. A *Freeman* writer called it a great show. J. E. Ogden, the sideshow manager, swore that Lowery's group was the best under canvas anywhere. Show veterans took disasters in stride: "The Hagenbeck-Wallace Shows came forth . . . slightly disfigured and a trifle crippled temporarily, but in a surprising brief period the organization pulled itself together, the proprietor had purchased more animals, the circus program was bettered, if such was possible, and the season of 1913 has left one trail of extremely favorable comment and eulogy all along the route—every stand people were emphatic in urging us to return next season and not to wait two years." That 1913 summer season was certainly memorable.[39]

LOWERY'S 1913–1914 DIXIE FASHION PLATE MINSTRELS

The Dixie Fashion Plate Minstrels opened their winter season in Mascoutah, Illinois, on November 23. The managers, J. R. Andrews and C. O. Gaines, had created the "finest equipped minstrel in every way that has ever struck the road." In addition to Gaines, Andrews, and Lowery, the company's roster included A. A. Wright, Thomas May, Elmer Payne, Anatole Victor, Mack Carter, Arthur Prince, Ruth Sprague Prince, Earl Granstaff, Al G. Fredericks, J. A. Johnson, William May, Tony Barfield, Eugene Peterson, Whitney Viney, Alex and Maybell Tolliver, Mather Glover, Carrie Gilbert, Callie Vassar, Daisy Webster, Nelson Hill, William Morris, M. Hoy, and Gordon Collins. Newspaper reporters from St. Louis, Chicago, Indianapolis, Kansas City, and Cincinnati attended the grand opening performance.[40]

The *Freeman* subsequently proclaimed that the show "opened in Mascoutah, Illinois, where we closed before—Jumped to St. Louis and copped barrels of dough. In fact they played the LaSalle Theater in St. Louis the entire week of December 1. Then they move on northwestward playing into Iowa—how good that does sound—New Year's in Clarinda, then Nebraska bound." Furthermore,

This season the Fashion Plate Minstrels are bigger, better, and grander than ever. Prof. Lowery boasts of the best minstrel band in the business. The new management believes in short parades, lively music, and flashy uniforms.

Our first part costumes are gorgeous; scenery is magnificent and quite a few gold instruments in the band. The performers and musicians are of the better class and live on a beautiful sleeper, "Ruth," just as one happy family. The show will go under canvas about April 15, and travel to Canada and the western states.[41]

In mid-January, they company reported that it had performed in the largest towns in Iowa, with the last week's shows of "banner" quality. Andrews was reportedly thinking about "opening up another company to tour Australia, China [and] France." Those thoughts certainly translated into incentive. "Mr. A. A. Wright, our stage director is very busy rehearsing a new afterpiece. . . . Mabelle Tolliver was seen rehearsing a new skating act. . . . Miss Carrie Gilbert is a very cute little lady monologist. . . . Tony Barefield is singing Jewell Johnson's late hit, "A Clinker Down in the Deep." . . . William Hay, the crack Indianapolis snare drummer has used up over twenty three drum heads this season."[42]

But the February 14 edition of the *Freeman* brought news that the show had not continued to prosper. First, the paper reported that Lowery veteran Arthur L. Prince had closed with the show and was in St. Louis. Second, "Owing to the scare of contagious disease, the Lowery–Dixie Fashion Plate Minstrel closed the season, Feb. 1st in Wellsville, Missouri. Everybody shook a hearty good-bye handshake. . . . P. G. Lowery is now booking for the season 1914 with the Wallace shows."[43] Thus came to a close what was perhaps Lowery's shortest professional performance season. Although no record of the illness survives, it apparently constituted enough of a scare to force a successful touring company off the road in midseason. There was no further mention of an overseas tour.

The shortened season gave Lowery and his performers an opportunity to pursue other endeavors. Some of the more than thirty members of the troupe probably sought employment in other shows; however, the press reported that "P. G. Lowery accompanied Billy and Tom May to their home in Wichita, Kans., and had a very pleasant trip. Billy and Tom May are visiting with P. G. Lowery on the farm, spending a pleasant vacation hunting and fishing." As usual, Lowery worked while he rested: the same article mentioned that he could place a few more musicians with the 1914 Wallace-Hagenbeck Show. Carrie Gilbert also apparently visited Lowery during this vacation.[44]

Lowery and his visitors left Reece on April 12, traveling via St. Louis to Indiana to prepare for the circus's April 21 opening. As he did every year, Lowery proclaimed the performers the best that he had ever had and announced his roster for the season: "I have re-engaged U. S. Thompson and Junk Edwards for first end men; Earl Granstaff and Amos Peoples second end men. They will be supported by Miss Carrie Gilbert, Callie Vassar, and Mrs. Jno. Edwards and a chorus of eight male voices. The band will consist of fourteen, the picked musicians, such as Elmer Payne, Robert Young, Thomas May, L[eslie] Davis, J. L. Edwards, A[natole] Victor, Amos Peoples, Jno. Tobias, Earl Granstaff, Jno. Haywood, Wm. May, Wm. Hoy. The orchestra will be conducted by the old reliable, A. Victor. I expect to carry 20 people this season."[45]

With this season, many things about the Hagenbeck-Wallace Show began to change. The new owners brought new ways of doing business. The circus opened its 1914 season two days earlier than it had the previous year and in a different locality. The winter quarters had moved from Peru to an area midway between French Lick and West Baden, Indiana. But as in previous years, the show emerged from its winter quarters in excellent form.

Mitchell, Ind., was the place selected for the dress rehearsals and preliminary opening. All went well and the program was rendered as if the troupe had been enroute for weeks. From the start the show was a very heavy one, there being a superfluity of acts, the dressing rooms being so crowded that performers were in each other's way.

The real opening occurred in Cincinnati, where four exhibitions were given. Again Cincinnati was very kind to us. . . . The performance and the parade were pronounced by the Cincinnati press as the best ever presented by this show, possibly by any circus.[46]

Other innovations were entering the circus world. One was electric lights, a sight that itself was worth the price of a ticket. The electric light-ing system made its debut during a night performance in Norwood, Ohio, wowing the audience, especially when the lights wet out for about fifteen seconds in the middle of the high wire act. Some performers fell, but no one was seriously hurt. According to reports, however, this was the only time that the lighting failed. Furthermore, the same night brought a rain-storm so severe that the show could not be loaded onto the train, which caused Hagenbeck-Wallace to miss its next scheduled performances in Middletown, Ohio.[47]

By late June, the circus had performed in Ohio, West Virginia, and Pennsylvania and was now in Indiana. Lowery's company added a few more players—James Jackson on drums, Al Fredericks on trombone and violin, Reuben Warren on baritone and trombone—and continued to receive royal treatment in various locations. The *Freeman* devoted plenty of ink to the welcome the company received from the Pittsburgh Elks, Iron City Lodge no. 77, an extravaganza that featured a sumptuous banquet dinner, addresses by the brothers, and instrumental and vocal entertainment. In addition, Lowery was initiated into the lodge. Lowery and company, in turn, put on a show that received rave reviews in the *Freeman* and the *Pittsburgh Press*.[48]

To earn such positive reviews, the show had to maintain its freshness and a uniqueness that would catch the audiences. Stage manager Junk Edwards received credit from the players for "framing up, what is said to be, the best minstrel under the white tops. He has divided [the performers] into three well-regulated shows, which makes it easier and more agreeable for all." Edwards's modifications were well received by audiences and the press as well.[49]

In September, the show stopped in Indianapolis, receiving positive reviews in the *Freeman*, which reported that Lowery "maintains the reputation of having the best show of the kind. The members of his company have been with him for several seasons and they have caught the Lowery spirit."[50]

With the arrival of October, members of the troupe began to plan for the winter season, rehearsing new acts and deciding where they would play. Some performers planned to go on the vaudeville circuit, while others hoped to remain with Lowery. The *Freeman* reported, "Amos Peoples is framing up some good stuff with a girl and they ought to be good. Mrs. Callie Vassar has some live songs for a sister team. She and her daughter, Miss Sophia Vassar, should have a hit. Lester Davis and Earl Granstaff have a musical novelty act that is different and new to the colored houses, rendering the classics and some real hot rags. Playing two cornets at once and dancing and playing trombone at [the] same time are their features, and they really do them. P. G. is looking over his boys while rehearsing, so you know they will be right."[51]

A SEASON WITH RICHARD AND PRINGLE'S MINSTRELS

During the winter season 1914–15, Lowery again headquartered in Columbus, Ohio. A January 1915 human-interest article written about him in the *Freeman* implied a degree of permanency to his Columbus residence. Furthermore, a subsequent story reported that Lowery had entered into a professional partnership with Billy Smith, manager of Columbus's Dunbar Theater, where Carrie Gilbert was performing that winter.[52]

Speculation began to grow about Lowery's plans for the coming summer circus season. Few newspaper items had appeared since October 1914, and rumors were plentiful. He reportedly had been hurt in a fall from a band-wagon during a parade, either in Eureka, Kansas, or in Indianapolis, and the injuries he suffered may have contributed to his indecision about his future plans. In April Lowery either remained undecided about what he wanted to do this season or was continuing to hold out for some unspecified offer. The *Freeman* reported that Lowery "had several offers under consideration for the coming season, but it is not known just what he will accept. It was thought that he would return to Wallace-Hagenbeck Circus as director of the famous colored band, but so far he seems undecided."[53]

The mystery concerning Lowery's immediate plans was resolved in May, when the surprising news appeared that he had assumed leadership of the Richard and Pringle's Minstrels Band. He gave no reason for his departure from Wallace-Hagenbeck. Joining Lowery in his new environment were Whitney Viney, William Hoy, Elmer Payne, and Irvin Richardson.[54]

People along the show's route often greeted Lowery with the adulation accorded a conquering hero, and he welcomed the opportunity to be of extraordinary service to them. When the Richard and Pringle show played in Thermopolis, Wyoming, the players heard of an older performer, Thomas Nickerson, and his wife, who lived there. Nickerson was paralyzed, and the family needed money. The members of the troupe considered making up a small purse from their personal resources but thought that doing so "would not show any great spirit of brotherly love to [Nickerson's] townspeople, who liked him to a person. . . . Clarence Powell suggested to P. G. Lowery and his generous band that they give a public [benefit] concert the next morning [and then take] up a public collection. As we did not leave until noon, we did so and a generous contribution was taken up and another invalid was made happy by a class of men who are not always looked upon favorably."[55]

The show was well received throughout its tour. A Deadwood, South Dakota, newspaper said, "Shows may come and shows may go, but Richard & Pringles' gets the business." In Fargo, North Dakota, the audiences were so large that people had to be turned away. Lowery "tried to get away with two solos nightly, but the clamor of the populace wouldn't stand for it, so as a third number he put on the Carnival of Venice, which is a nightly hit." In July, however, the troupe received the sad news that James Hall, a long-time euphonium player in Lowery's band, had died.[56.]

After completing the western leg of their tour, the minstrels headed back east, where they had a variety of performance dates, including some in Kansas. In Topeka, George N. Jackson and his band gave Lowery and his company a "Grand reception," with refreshments, toasts, and a short concert by Jackson's band, "which was heartily applauded by the minstrel company and the large crowd that gathered to welcome P. G. back to his birthplace."[57]

Lowery continued to hone his band and his show. In late November, in Pasadena, California, he added trombonist Fay Williams and tuba player George K. Lyde. Manzie Campbell returned to the show after a bereavement leave, and in late December, Moses McQuitty joined the troupe. Lowery continually added new music to his group's performance repertoire so that there were "enough overtures at his command to play a different concert each night for a week." Said the *Freeman* correspondent, "Whitney Viney, our efficient stage director, by adding something new here and there, and touching up weak spots, has given us a show of two and a half hours' entertainment without a weak spot in it, and one enjoyed by all who see it."[58]

As the show moved into Texas in February 1916, the fans were excited about Lowery's big band. Fountain B. Woods, a trombonist who had played with Lowery at the turn of the century, rejoined the group, and Lowery added Henry Paschal, a clarinetist, and Walter Mason, a cornetist. Trap drummer Kid Hoy closed and was replaced by J. W. Wright. Said the

Freeman, "P. G. Lowery's big concert band now numbers about twenty able musicians, and the professor says he'll not stop until he has twenty-seven. His band now includes four saxophones and two oboes, and when they get through with the daily concert you can't hear anything but words of praise, and why not? Isn't the great P. G. Lowery at the helm? That's the answer."[59] During his forty-eight weeks heading the Richard and Pringle's Minstrels, Lowery built a formidable show.

RETURN TO HIS FIRST LOVE

In late March 1916, the *Freeman* announced that "P. G. Lowery is again with his first love, the Hagenbeck-Wallace Shows, this season." At long last, the paper also offered an explanation about why he left: "It may prove to be interesting information to know the cause of his leaving the Hagenbeck-Wallace Circus in 1915. He refused the engagement because the manager requested his men to double canvas. P. G. informed the manager he would leave [the show before his men would] double canvas, and at once notified his band of his firm stand, and the same was heartily endorsed by his band, and every band director in the circus business—such as Mr. Wolfscales, [Rob Roy] Pope, James Harris and others." Thus, Lowery had left Hagenbeck-Wallace because the new management wanted his musicians and performers to do what was considered the work of laborers or roustabouts, raising and tearing down the circus tents. Lowery's stance had the backing of the sideshow directors of the other major circuses—Barnum and Bailey's Wolfscales, Ringling Brothers' Pope, and Gollmar Brothers' Harris—as well as the attention of the national black news media and the respect of the African-American showgoers nationwide. Having resolved the matter to his satisfaction, Lowery rejoined Hagenbeck-Wallace and announced in typical fashion that he "expects to have the best band and minstrel show he has ever carried and has the best wishes of everybody."[60]

His return was well met: in late May or early June, "When P. G. Lowery arrived in Mitchell, Ind., to open with the H & W Circus he was greeted by hundreds of performers who were glad to see him back." The band's roster included Tom May and Charles Creath, cornets; William Moore, first alto; Irvin Richardson, second alto; Lafayette Williams and Ed Carr, trombones; John Eubanks, baritone; Tony Barefield, singer and bass player; William May; bass; Elmer Payne, solo clarinet; Maylon Hall, first clarinet and tenor singer; William Hoy, snare drum and bells; and Jackie Smith, who sang baritone and played bass drum. The orchestra featured William Moore, violin and leader; Lafayette Williams, violin; Thomas May, cornet; Edward Carr, trombone, William May, bass; and William Hoy, trap drums. The singers and soubrettes were Essie Williams, Mrs. Charles Creath, and Irvin Richardson, and comedian Happy Kimball also joined the troupe.[61]

The company also had a veteran performer with a new name: Carrie Gilbert Lowery. Sometime between the 1914–15 and 1915–16 seasons, Gilbert and Lowery had married. Their relationship was perhaps one of the circuit's best-kept secrets. Although Gilbert had performed with Lowery's enterprise continuously beginning in 1908 and had visited Reece, no real hints of any romantic involvement emerged until their marriage was announced. Observers had believed that the traveling minstrels were Lowery's family.[62]

As on previous tours, Lowery and his troupe received a warm welcome in many of the places they visited, including Youngstown, Columbus, and Dayton, Ohio; and Connellsville and Coatesville, Pennsylvania. The group's performances were also extremely well received. And while playing in Danville, they performed another act of public service, visiting the state penitentiary at the warden's invitation.[63] While there is no state penitentiary in Danville, Indiana, the Plainfield Correctional Center is approximately 20 miles from Danville. This is probably where Lowrey played.[64]

August, the season's middle, found Lowery planning for the winter tour and focusing on his personnel. The *Freeman* reported that Lowery "expects to enlarge his company now for the theatrical season that will open at the close of the circus season. Lowery can place a few more people now. Good baritone for the band; also [a] comedian and dancers; violinist who doubles in band can be placed immediately."[65]

During September, Eubanks left to return to school, and Kimball also closed. The September 16 issue of the *Freeman* reported the group's roster as "P. G. Lowery, cornet and director; Thomas May, cornet, band and orchestra: W. Fields, cornet and baritone; Elmer Payne, clarinet, band and orchestra; Maylon Hall, clarinet, 2nd tenor; Dan White, baritone and violin; Edgar Carr, trombone, band and orchestra; Irvie Richardson, alto and 1st tenor; Wm. May, tuba, band and orchestra; Tony Barfield, tuba and bass solo; Wm. Hoy, trap drums; Jackie Smith, bass drum and comedian; Bennie Jones, principal comedian; Mrs. Essie Williams, soprano, Mrs. Carrie Lowery, soprano."[66]

Hagenbeck-Wallace closed its 1916 season at Mount Carmel, Illinois, on October 25. The *Freeman* reported that all members of Lowery's company had made arrangements for the winter season. P. G. and Carrie Lowery, Essie Williams, William and Thomas May, and Elmer Payne were going to spend the winter in Columbus, Ohio; Jackie Smith was headed for Chicago; Bennie Jones was going to be stage manager with Allen's Minstrels; and Dan White was to become band and orchestra leader for Harry Rowe. Going along with White were Maylon Hall, Irvie Richardson, Edgar Carr and William Hoy.[67]

The marketing drumbeat for Lowery's 1917 season began in January of that year. Because this was the start of only the second season since Lowery's stint with Richard and Pringle's Minstrels, the Hagenbeck-Wallace Circus went to great lengths to reassure the public that during the coming season, "P. G. Lowery will be identified with the Hagenbeck-Wallace Shows." The *Freeman* also reported that to induce Lowery to return, Hagenbeck-Wallace had "arranged the finest sleeping [car] ever occupied by Colored companies with a circus." Through March, subsequent issues of the *Freeman* kept Lowery's name before its readers, with items noting visitors to his home, a new march dedicated to him, his expectations for the coming season, and the number of musicians and performers who would join his company. On March 24, the newspaper announced, "P. G. Lowery will carry a larger band and minstrel this season than any previous season, and he has used great care in selecting the very best talent. The roster will appear later. He can place a few more good musicians, especially trombone and clarinets to double."[68]

The 1917 season and show opened with Hagenbeck-Wallace at Indianapolis on April 18. Lowery's band consisted of Lowery, owner, supervisor, cornet, and leader; Thomas May, Charles Creath, and Robert Stevenson, cornets; James Berry and John Mayfield, trombones; James F. Faulkner and Charles Beechum, drums; Maylon Hall and D. W. Batsell, clarinets; William Moore and Mack Carter, alto horns; Arthur C. Cobb, baritone euphonium; and William May, tuba. The orchestra was led by Moore and featured Batsell on clarinet, Tom May on cornet, Berry on trombone, William May on bass, and Faulkner on drums. In addition to his instrumental duties, Beechum served as stage manager, performed as an end man, and sang. The other performers included end men Jackie Smith, Mack Carter, and Charles Creath; Callie Vassar Hill, interlocutor; and vocalists Olga Beechum, Carrie Lowery, and Jackie Smith.[69]

After playing Indianapolis, the Hagenbeck-Wallace Show traveled to Columbus, Ohio, where Lowery took the company to his home and feted them with a banquet. Then, during the show's stand in Parkersburg, West Virginia, on May 3,

Prof. Zack McClung assisted by his excellent band, arranged a grand reception for P. G. Lowery and his entire company. The company was escorted to the A.M.E. church where Prof. McClung rendered an excellent concert of classical, popular and ragtime music. The band was very liberal in responding to several encores. The entire audience showed their appreciation to the progress of the band, as the music was nicely rendered by the band. P. G. pronounced the band one of the best in West Virginia.

After the concert, the band boys escorted Lowery and his band to their beautiful apartments known as the Magnolia apartments, where refreshments were served in abundance and everybody had an enjoyable time.[70]

In late May, the weather became somewhat inhospitable, especially in Michigan. Batsell wrote to the *Freeman*, "The weather is very cold—every day looks like snow. This has been a very bad season on the tent shows, but we have never missed a performance. Saturday, May 26, while parading at Lansing, Mich., we were caught in a fearful hailstorm and the boys had a hard time trying to dodge the large hailstones; some were as large as hen eggs. Luckily there was no damage. After the hail storm a shower of rain followed, which gave the boys a good soaking. Lansing will be long remembered." The rough weather seemed to dog the show—although the troupe had yet to miss a performance going into the sixth week of the tour, a cyclone passed close by while Hagenbeck-Wallace was in Winchester, Indiana. Batsell also reported a "little accident on our No. 2 section Tuesday morning, May 29, just before leaving Ann Arbor, Mich., for Detroit, a flat car ran on a derail[er] and was turned over, smashing the big band wagon, calliope, the $10,000 mystery auto wagon." Other misfortunes included the illness of Charles Creath, who was stricken with rheumatism and had to close with the show at St. Louis.[71]

Lowery did something unique during this tour. Because circus workers all have assigned tasks during the shows, they rarely, if ever, get to see the performances. But Lowery, "with his band and minstrels, entertained the employees of the H & W with two and a half hours' of minstrels and vaudeville at Perry, Iowa, July 1. Everyone voted [it] the best ever. The show was staged by Charles Beechum, Jakie Smith and Mack Carter, Prof. Lowery, soloist, and Prof. William Moore, leader of [the] orchestra."[72]

The show spent July and August touring the West before returning to Iowa late in the summer. Batsell summarized the western trek for the *Freeman*'s readers:

After spending three weeks in the far West we are now back in civilization once more. The fine scenery of the Rocky Mountains was enjoyed by all, but the sands of Wyoming and Montana were a nuisance and made each day on the plains miserable. Mr. Roberson, trombonist will leave for his home in South Dakota Monday, August 27. . . . Mr. S. B. Foster, violin and cornet, of the Big Six fame, Greenwood, Miss., will soon join us. . . . Prof. P. G. Lowery visited his home last Wednesday August 15, and reports an enjoyable time. His farm is located in the center of the great oil belt of Kansas and we are liable to hear of a new oil magnate at any time. Mr. Charles Beechum, our stage manager, has a No. 1 show.[73]

Although the return to the east reflected the show's continued success, Lowery was again planning ahead for the winter season. He intended to team up with R. M. Harvey, business manager of the Hagenbeck-Wallace Circus, to front a new "colored" minstrel show called Lowery's Greater Minstrels. The circus's Al G. Hoffman and Charles Feeney would serve as managers. According to the *Freeman*, "carrying thirty-five people, the company . . . will play Northern territory only, opening shortly after the closing of the circus season."[74]

LOWERY'S GREATER MINSTRELS

The Hagenbeck-Wallace show closed in West Baden, Indiana, on October 23. The *Freeman* had already announced that all performers engaged for Lowery's Greater Minstrels should report for rehearsals on October 29 in St. Louis. This call also indicated that "Mr. R. M. Harvey, owner of these Minstrels, agrees to pay boarding expenses during [the] week of rehearsal." This was a startling luxury, with more to come.

When the members of the Lowery Greater Minstrels assembled in St. Louis for rehearsal, they soon realized that these minstrels have plenty of money back of them, and then soon were given to understand that they were to be with a real troupe, one that was equipped to play the largest cities as well as the small ones. The wardrobe is said by the boys to eclipse anything they ever saw with a minstrel, black or white. The scenery is all new and according to original ideas. The dressing of the first part affords an extraordinary chance for wardrobe display, while the car on which the company will live is fit for a king. Evidently, Mr. Harvey is going to adopt the standard of the Hagenbeck Circus when it comes to class and quality both as to equipment, organization and performance. Professor Lowery . . . and all the other celebrities are enthusiastic.[75]

Lowery's Greater Minstrels opened the season on November 5, 1917, in Fulton, Missouri. Money and resources seemed to be both unrestricted and unlimited, and the show was

conceded by press and public to be America's foremost minstrel. When you are told that two [railroad] cars are jammed and packed with scenery, people, baggage and automobiles (for the parades), you can by infinite imagination, get a slight idea how sixty people, not including the executive staff of eight looks to the natives in the various towns we visit.

The parade is headed by Miss Johuella Williams, the only colored lady buglist in the business, mounted on a snow white Arabian steed, purchased from one of America's leading circuses for the show by Mr. Harvey, followed by Mr. R. M. Harvey, Al Hoffman and C. A. Pheeney in an automobile, walking gents of twenty, and fourteen girls in four autos, winding up with Prof. Lowery's band of 28 colored musicians. Positively the largest colored band traveling in America today, and as all know P. G. Lowery and his aim, that is to have at all times the very best he can. Without any wide stretch of the imagination, imagine what the band must be.

Now the show which was written and staged by that well-known comedian, Ed Tolliver, whose experience in the show business here and abroad has fitted him to give Lowery's Greater Minstrels that finishing touch that all successful shows must have, artistic touches and knock-out climaxes to all parts of the show, in a manner unsurpassed by any other latter day producers. Headed by Clarence Powell, the well-known star and Ed Tolliver as co-star, connected with such well-known artists as Frank Kirk, Watts Brothers, Means and Means, Jakie Smith, Walter Robinson, Irvin Richardson, James Thomas, Curly Johnson, Whitmore and Whitmore, Edna Barrett, Callie Vassar, Johnella Williams, Mina Johnson are a few of the many bright lights that shine nightly; while the orchestra is under the able direction of Samuel R. Paste."[76]

Lowery's Greater Minstrels received "thunderous applause," "having the best of everything, and delivering the goods." Wrote the *Freeman*, "That [the] permanently distinct and perennial style of amusement known as 'the minstrel' is still popular with the masses is conclusively proven by the enormous business done by that company of standard excellence, Lowery's Greater Minstrels, and if the voice of the press and public may be taken as a criterion, the show this year is by far the best show that ever bore the name of America's foremost cornettist, P. G. Lowery." But the tour did not proceed without incident. On November 14, a fire broke out in the women's dressing room while the troupe performed in Trenton, Missouri, resulting in the loss of some costume parts and of some of the performers' street clothes. The December 22 edition of the *Freeman* reported that the company was encountering "zero weather" in such places as Albert Lea, Minnesota, but indicated that adversity was offset by the fact that the company was very comfortable riding in a nicely heated railroad car and performing in cozy theaters. The show also lost its drummer, Kid Hoy, who went home because of the death of his mother.[77]

WORLD WAR I: EFFORTS AND EFFECTS

U.S. involvement in World War I began to affect Lowery's performance itinerary by limiting the show's ability to travel. Railroad embargos and other restrictions on movement that were intended to assist the war effort may have adversely affected many shows, including Lowery's new Greater Minstrels. Some shows closed down almost immediately, while others devised ways to complete at least some parts of their seasons.

In January 1918, a well-known theater owner, manager, and showman, S. H. Dudley, visited Lowery's troupe in Brooklyn, Iowa, and was impressed, as indicated by his review, which appeared in the *Freeman* on January 5. Dudley particularly noted the show's wardrobe and the singing of Joe Means, Jackie Smith, and Clarence Powell. Of Lowery, Dudley wrote, "anyone can see that . . . Lowery is still the greatest cornetist of our race, and he knows how to make you like it." In summary, Dudley said, "it was a damn good show."[78]

But just a week later, the *Freeman* printed an article entitled "Government Closes Shows": "On account of the serious condition of railroads not being able to transport government supplies and materials as rapidly as was necessary, [an] embargo was placed on all shows using private cars and classed as nonessentials. All amusements of this class were forced to close for the present, if not temporarily until the war has been brought to an end."[79]

This situation seriously challenged the road shows. One creative show owner announced that he would travel using three trucks and several automobiles. J. C. O'Brien, proprietor of C. O'Brien's Georgia Minstrels, took a legal approach, as he and several colleagues petitioned the railroad commission and other regulatory entities. Perhaps as a result of these appeals, the embargo was brief: the February 9 *Freeman* also carried a story headed, "After Ten Days Tie-Up Tent Shows Move over the Railroads." However, this story offers no information concerning the level and availability of railroad service for private cars for the duration of the war.[80]

By late March, the show continued and was running into circus season schedules, although the *Freeman* made no mention of the usual shift from winter to summer venues. Clarence Powell's report on Lowery's Greater

Minstrels in the March 23 *Freeman* contained primarily human-interest items, including the news that Alonzo Moore, "the world's greatest magician," had joined the show in Kansas City. This issue of the newspaper also contained Lowery's ad for musicians, comedians, and dancers for the troupe. In April, the *Freeman* urged performers to "make your applications early for the summer tour through Canada with Lowery's Greater Minstrels."[81]

"Notes from Lowery's Greater Minstrels," published in the May 4 *Freeman*, also said nothing about the show related to the circus season. Lowery and his performers were giving successful shows in leading theaters in the vicinity of Minneapolis and St. Paul, Minnesota. Personnel additions included George Barton, who took over as manager as a result of R. M. Harvey's illness; James Berry, a trombone virtuoso; and Anna Henderson, a soubrette. Said the *Freeman*, "P. G. Lowery's Band is increasing in numbers by leaps and bounds."[82]

On May 11, the *Freeman* carried an ad for "Prof L. K. Baker's Annex with [the] Hagenbeck-Wallace Circus." Lowery would not rejoin the circus but would continue with his Greater Minstrels, currently playing in Illinois and Indiana. On June 1, the Greater Minstrels advertised for performers for a "Far Western Tour."[83]

Although the reasons that Lowery did not join Hagenbeck-Wallace during the 1918 season were not published, the situation turned out to have been fortuitous for Lowery, enabling him and his performers to miss the "great circus train wreck of 1918" at Ivanhoe Tower, Indiana. The Hagenbeck-Wallace Show had become so large that it was "carried by three special trains, it had 22 tents and 1,000 employees on the weekly payroll." Equipment would be struck and loaded onto trains as soon as it was no longer needed, so the circus traveled in three separate train units, or sections. All three sections had been loaded and were en route from Michigan City, Indiana, to Hammond, Indiana, when on June 22, "Thirty-seven employees of the Hagenbeck-Wallace Circus were killed about 4 this morning, when the second section of the circus train, on the Michigan Central [Railroad] was crashed into by an empty troop train near Burr Street and 9th Avenue, at Gary Gardens. Both trains were going west. Most of the dead were burned to death in the fire, which started in the wooden sleepers of the circus train immediately after the wreck." Despite the tragedy, the remnants of the Hagenbeck-Wallace Show played in Beloit, Wisconsin, on June 25.[84]

Lowery's Greater Minstrels closed in August, "owing to railroad conditions." Lowery indicated that he hoped to reopen "under new management in the near future" and headed to Nitro, West Virginia, where he conducted a community band at the powder plant. In support of the war effort, "two bands were organized [at the plant] and were made up of professional bandsmen from across the nation. The colored band had 36 pieces and played at Liberty Loan Drives, band concerts and many other occasions." According to the *Freeman*, the band was managed by Harley Baker and directed by Lowery. The performers included "clarinets, P. A. Lambert, V. R. Dixon, C. H. Smith, C. Williams; cornets, W. Johnson, H. Franklin, R. Jasper, H. Alexander (saxophone); altos, W. Watson, H. Shaddon; trombones, F. Miller, H. Scipio, G. Dishroom; baritones, R. Warren (trombone), G. McDonald, A. Hews (violin); saxophones, C. Hicks, W Coleman (alto); basses, R. Wilson, H. May; drums, H. Baker, C. Reed. O. Kendall (piano), S. Ewing."[85] By the end of September, Lowery's band was receiving wide acceptance and performed regularly. The *Freeman* reported that

Lowery is meeting with great success in Nitro, W. Va., with his concert band of 30 picked musicians. His winning disposition and ability as a director has won him thousands of friends at this Government plant. The various music houses all over the U.S. were quick to locate P. G.'s whereabouts (as he is commonly called) and every mail has a bunch of music fresh from the press. The band gives two concerts each week, which is largely attended and enjoyed by every one. The programmes are changed each concert and are always arranged in a style so as to please every one. The band has five first-class soloists who appear by turns each concert and they play from rags to standard music. Mr. Harley Baker, the manager of the band, considers himself very lucky to secure such a director as Mr. Lowery.

Perhaps an even greater accolade came in the form of a letter of commendation from Roscoe Marriner Floyd, the president of the Boston Conservatory, Lowery's alma mater. The letter stated that "After listening to the concert by the Nitro Colored Concert Band I am thoroughly convinced a body of colored musicians under good training can render classical music as well as our best white bands."[86]

World War I officially came to its conclusion on November 11, 1918, ending the restrictions on traveling shows. On December 21, the *Freeman* offered the first information regarding Lowery's postwar plans: "Prof. P. G. Lowery, the noted band leader . . . will be with the Ringling Brothers and Barnum and Bailey Circuses Combines the coming season."[87]

WINDJAMMIN' WITH THE RINGLINGS—THE CLEVELAND CONNECTION

After the war, Lowery changed both his home and his place of employment. According to Lowery's recollection, he joined the Ringling Brothers Circus on April 16, 1919, and remained with them until September 12, 1931. While with the "Big Bertha" (the nickname for the Ringling Brothers show), Lowery generally served as conductor and of course played cornet. Other band members included Al Kemp and R. C. Hicks, trumpets; Bill Matthews, clarinet and sax; Howard Duffy, slide trombone; Bill Fisher, baritone; Bill May, bass horn; Eddie Warren and Rufus Dixon, drums and traps.[88]

When the Ringling Brothers and Barnum and Bailey Combined Shows opened in New York, *Billboard* magazine announced that the primary annex attraction under the sideshow canvas was "P. P. [*sic*] Lowery and his band of eighteen musicians and minstrels [who] will hold forth on the stage, horseshoed by eighteen platforms, and in the center a special 'steel bound' arena will house Congo and Sallie, the strange jungle companions." This description of the sideshow's physical setup gives only a hint of the attractions. The process began not inside the tent but outside, on the midway.

The sideshow manager gets up on the platform, the bally stand, and starts talking to the audience. That's called the "tip," and he is making a thing called the first opening. And he would say [something to the effect that] "Now, the main show isn't going to start for an hour. You've got lots of time, and you won't miss anything, and you want to come in here to the sideshow. In the meantime we're going to bring out some attractions." . . . Then they would bring out—oh, say, a lady with a snake or one of the attractions from the sideshow. Then the snake charmer would get up on the platform and this was the ballyhoo to attract a crowd.

Between the tent and the bally stand would be P. G. Lowery's band. They would be in uniform. He had a kind of a flat-top cap, a beaked cap, and they would all be in their band uniforms. And I guess that he would probably have six or eight people there. [The sideshow manager] had a gravel voice—you know [he was] a talker, a barker. And out of the side of his mouth as a cue, he would say, "Bally P. G.!" And just like turning off a switch, the band would come to life, and P. G. would quit talking . . . and start playing just instantaneously. They'd play some fast kind of Dixieland, probably, do several bars of that, then stop. And the sideshow manager would pick up again with his talking.[89]

The second segment would be the inside portion of the show. Patrons were enticed into entering the sideshow tent to view more of the mysteries and marvels therein.

The sideshow talker made his second opening—in other words, tried again to get people to buy tickets. People would go to the ticket sellers, which were in boxes at each end of the banner lines [pictures that showed attractions in the show]. Incidentally, one of those canvas pictures would be about P. G. Lowery and his minstrel band, or some other such billing as that. . . .

When the talker, the sideshow manager, went into the tent to start that performance, [the audience] would go from one platform to another. On each platform was one of these attractions: the fat lady, a midget, or whatever. At one end of this tent would be a bigger platform, and that is where the band would perform. Now, the band would be outside for that bally, . . . then when the show manager comes in, the band would trail in with him and get on this bandstand. Then they would play, particularly when the—they called him a "sideshow orator"—he would take the crowd from each of these bally stands, each of these platforms, to the next one. When they got to the one with the band, then that sideshow band would play Dixieland music and the dancers would dance. They would do two or three numbers as a minstrel show [without] end men.[90]

The members of the crowd would move from stand to stand until they had circled the tent. The barker, the band, and some of the sideshow attractions would then repeat the same process with a new audience.

This format apparently provided a good mix for Lowery's show. *Billboard* magazine quoted writer Lew Graham as saying, "P. G. Lowery's Band is the best side show band in America. They play a repertoire that ranges from operatic overtures to the latest jazz. They look resplendent in the new uniforms of blue piped with red and gold." Lowery's connection with the Big Bertha seemed to result in a certain pride: he had arrived at the pinnacle of show success. On August 2, 1919, the *Freeman* announced, "Prof. P. G. Lowery and his celebrated band will be in Indianapolis August 18th with Ringling Brothers and Barnum & Bailey Shows. Nuf sed." Before reaching Indianapolis, the circus played in Chicago from August 9 to 17, and while there, Lowery advertised that he was always looking to improve and encouraged "discharged musicians from the army" to contact him. Lowery and his troupe were welcomed in both Chicago and Indianapolis, where they were greeted "by thousands of friends and admirers."[91]

When Lowery arrived in Topeka for a September 3 show, he received a hero's welcome that included a sumptuous reception and concert. After Topeka, the circus performed in Wichita. Lowery then made a quick trip home to Reece to visit his mother and check on the farm before rejoining the show in Oklahoma City.[92]

Like the 1918 Hagenbeck-Wallace Circus, the 1919 Ringling Brothers traveled in several train sections. On September 15, one of the sections had an accident in or near Okmulgee, Oklahoma, that resulted in the loss of fourteen horses, the destruction of four stock cars, and injuries to two workers. The performers were all unhurt, and by October 24, the *Freeman* reported that "everything [is] running smoothly again, the band is in good condition and all are enjoying the best of health."[93]

The Ringlings closed their 1919 season show on November 21 after playing Savannah, Georgia. Despite challenges related to the smaller pool of available musicians as a result of World War I and to "prevailing circumstances," Lowery's band had a complete roster from opening to closing. Lowery and his troupe traveled "forty-three thousand miles . . . covering thirty states and visiting all of the principal cities of the United States." A December 13 *Freeman* headline read, "P. G. Lowery's Engagement with the Ringling Brothers and Barnum & Bailey's Combined Shows a Decided

Success—Re-Engaged for 1920." The same issue of the newspaper enthused about the abilities of Lowery's performers:

Clarinet player . . . D. W. Batsell [is] a very competent musician, arranger and composer and a master of the reed section. . . . Thomas May . . . has held the cornet seat and assistant leader for some years. Arthur Fields, a pupil of Mr. Lowery, on cornet, was called away before the close of the season. Richard Jasper, the Huntington, [W.] Va. Cornetist, formerly a member of Lowery's Concert Band of Nitro, W. Va., opened and closed with the show and proved himself a real trouper. Mr. Carl Boddy, a young cornetist, of Everett, Pa., took particular advantage of the schooling . . . made it a daily study and showed the greatest advancement of any in the band. The alto section was ably handled by Mr. L. B. Herenlow and Gordon Holland, both experienced in the music world, and they both dealt out the harmony both musical and personal. The troubadour [trombone] section was at first handled by Mr. James Herry and Redus Horton. . . . Their places were [subsequently] filled by Mr. A. H. Bass of St. Louis; Zoo Robinson, of New Orleans, and Bishop Dorsey of Chicago. The trombones proved to be a feature of the band. Arthur Cobb of Columbus, O., a former member of Lowery's Band did himself credit [playing] baritone. Cobb has a bright future before him in the music world. It is useless to speak [of] the bass. Just the word "Billy May" is sufficient. His experience and careful study has placed him in a class by himself. . . .

James Faulkner, another old member of Lowery's Band, was found again behind the bass drum and he is one of the few colored bass drummers who can read drum music and play drums, while Richard Murphy, of Dayton, O., manipulated the snare drum.

Our entertainers were Mrs. Carrie Lowery, the singing soubrette, who deserves special mention for the reputation she made for work, dress, and her conduct, paved the way so others could follow. Richard Murphy, known as "Dusty," was the champion buck and wing dancer. Mr. John Sloan was also a stage attraction, known as the one-man jazz band.[94]

Barely a month later, Lowery advertised in the *Freeman* for "experienced musicians on all instruments, cornets, clarinets, baritones, trombones, also high class singing and dancing comedians that double in band."[95] At this time, Lowery remained a resident of Columbus. However, sometime shortly thereafter, he moved his off-season headquarters to Cleveland.

From the late nineteenth century through about 1925, Cleveland was a center for black culture, particularly instrumental and vocal music, and would have had abundant attractions for a musician of Lowery's stature. According to George W. Brown, "When the Original Georgia Minstrels appeared at Brainard's Hall, March 26 and 27 in 1872, they so fascinated the public that a few local Negro musicians joined them. Furthermore, as early as 1898, Cleveland had an organized black band, Excelsior, under the direction of Charles McAfee.⁹⁶

Since 1907, Cleveland had had a local lodge of the Elks, the largest black fraternal organization. These groups furnished an outlet for the energies of the African-American community and helped to maintain high morale and provide bonding and fellowship. The Elks and other such lodges commonly sponsored one or more bands and numerous singers.⁹⁷

Although the specific date when Lowery moved to Cleveland is unknown, he was involved with bands there as early as January 1920, when a he auditioned and critiqued three of the city's bands, the Ladies' Silver Leaf Band (sometimes called the Silver Seal Band), the Jackson Military Band, and the Excelsior Band. Lowery reported to the *Freeman* that

I feel it my duty to let the readers of the Freeman know that Cleveland musicians comprise a large body of broad-minded, helpful and ambitious musicians. I was invited to visit a rehearsal of each band and several orchestras, which I accepted with pleasure.

The first was . . . the Silver Leaf Ladies' Band comprising 20 of the leading ladies of Cleveland under the directorship of Prof. Smith, a very able instructor. The band rendered a program . . . consisting of marches, overtures, waltzes, etc., that was a credit to any band. Special mention is due to the . . . solo cornet, horns and baritone[s], and the other ladies [also] did credit to their parts.

The second band to visit was the Jackson Military Band under the leadership of Prof. A. Walden. This band had a membership of 35 good musicians and from the program rendered, it showed [that] great care and patience had brought the band to this high standard by Prof. Walden.

The last, but not the least was the Excelsior Band. The membership is not as large as the other band but their playing was excellent and [they] rendered a very high class program consisting of overtures, marches and one number that deserved special mention: a tuba solo that displayed great skill by the rapid execution and tonal qualities. Prof. U. J. Hawlond, the Director, should feel proud from the result of his efforts in the music field.[98]

When not traveling with the circus during the 1920s, Lowery spent his time in Cleveland, "where he conducted a music studio and worked with community groups during the winter." Lowery also directed bands sponsored by the Elks' organization, including the Ladies' Silver Seal Band and a male band.[99]

On March 25, 1920, the Ringling Brothers and Barnum and Bailey Combined Shows would open a [five to six] week run at Madison Square Garden in New York. On March 20, the *Freeman* announced that "Lowery's Band will be one of the features in the Grand Entry and will take part in the performance." This represented a major development, the first time that a black band would play under the big top. Merle Evans, director of the Ringling Brothers' big-top band, had been instrumental in Lowery's hiring for the Ringling sideshow. Evans also wanted Lowery's group to play with Evans's white band under the big top. According to historian William H. Rehrig, "When Merle Evans became bandmaster of the Ringling Brothers and Barnum & Bailey Circus in 1919, he asked Lowery to lead the side show [and] attempted to have [Lowery] transferred to the big top band, but he was denied because of racial segregation." Fred Jewell Jr., the son of a composer and circus band director, quoted his father as saying that "the Negro bandsmen played only in the sideshows, despite their talent. . . . Neither the [white] bandsmen nor show management would consider hauling down the segregation barrier." But in 1920, nearly unnoticed, Lowery broke an old circus tradition. On April 17, the *Freeman* noted that Lowery's group had become the "first Colored band to play a feature number in any big show."[100]

As evidenced by the attempt to have Lowery play with the big-top band, Evans greatly respected Lowery's musicianship. Late in his life, Evans recalled that Lowery could "blow that horn! A first-rate musician. . . . When he and his gang blasted off for the bally, well, that was sure enough windjammin.'"[101]

According to the *Freeman*, Lowery had "a well-balanced band of picked musicians" this season: William Blue Jr. on clarinet; Thomas May,

R. Q. Dickerson, and Richard Jasper on cornet; Charles Evans, Ed Tolliver, and James Young on alto; Redus Horton, H. M. Lankford, and A. H. Bass on trombone; Winston Walker and Alvin "Zoo" Robertson on baritone; Walter Coleman on saxophone; William May on bass; and Walter Coleman, Victor Miller, and James Holmes on drums. The vocalist was Carrie Lowery.[102]

P. G. Lowery became an even more highly visible public figure, with his professional and social comings and goings printed in the newspapers. And now that Lowery was associated with the biggest name in show business, some people attempted to connect themselves to him for commercial purposes. For example, the publishing industry sought to attach its products to Lowery by implying that other bands could play like Lowery's by using certain music. On May 8, 1920, the *Freeman* printed a thinly disguised ad subtitled "P. G. Lowery's Band Featured Two New Skidmore Song Hits": according to this "article," "P. G. Lowery, the greatest colored bandmaster of the greatest Jazz band in the world is featuring two Skidmore song hits for this season. Carrie Lowery is singing them to patrons of the world's biggest circus—Ringling Brothers–Barnum Bailey. Carrie sings both to a fare thee well and the writer who heard her thinks these are both world beater songs, entitled "I'm Gonna Jazz My Way Right through Paradise," and "Never Let No One Man Worry Your Mind." These can be obtained for late program and stamps, from Skidmore Music Co., Gaiety Theater Bldg., 1847 Broadway, New York." Similarly, the May 22 *Freeman* carried an ad stating that "Arthur L. Prince, Bandmaster [is] Teaching the P. G. Lowery Broad-Tone Method with F. C. Wolcott's Rabbit Foot Minstrels." Prince had worked with Lowery on the Fashion Plate Minstrels, and this less-than-subtle attempt sought to imply that Prince could teach his students to play like Lowery.[103]

As had been the case in previous years, Lowery's band was warmly received in cities all along its route. Receptions were held for the troupe in Washington, D.C.; Pittsburgh; Cleveland; Indianapolis; Chicago; Milwaukee; Minneapolis; Kansas City, Missouri; Birmingham, Alabama; and many other places. At other stops, local bands would meet the show train and serenade Lowery and his performers. The show closed on October 27, after playing in Richmond, Virginia, the last stop on a thirty-state tour that the *Freeman* called "the most successful season experienced by P. G. Lowery and his band."[104]

Lowery had created what was the best circus sideshow band and was employed by the Greatest Show on Earth. He was undoubtedly riding the crest of his career. In 1921, *Billboard* magazine printed an article by J. A. Jackson concerning African-American entertainers, including Lowery and his band. According to Jackson,

Prof. P. G. Lowery and his band, for twenty-one years a feature of the bigger circuses, is probably known to more people than any other of the long list of Negro musical organizations that have long since become established parts of the circus business. This band is one of the institutions of the big show. He is now with the Ringlings.

Its success is almost entirely due to the rigid discipline maintained by Mr. Lowery as being equally essential with a high professional standard for its members. Yet, he is no martinet. He is a mild-mannered man who assumes no airs, nor does he intrude himself into notice other than such as his professional abilities attract. In spite of this modesty he has received many compliments from folks high in the world's official life.

A September 1922 review of Lowery's show in Los Angeles stated, "P. G. had one of the best bands in the business; in fact, the best I've ever heard under canvas. They could play everything from ragtime to opera, everything from jazz to overtures, and made the natives like it." The 1922 edition of the band contained many of the same performers, with some new names mixed in: Tom May, Stanley Elliott, Richard Jasper, James Faulkner, William Matthews Jr., Calvin A. Ivory, Hardy L. Arlington, James Holmes, Winston Walker, Charles W. Evans, William May, Percy Lee, and James Bank. These musicians, who played while wearing brilliant red, blue, and gold uniforms, constituted the best sideshow band in America.[105]

THE LOWERY BROTHERS CIRCUS?

In 1924, P. G. Lowery pulled off another unusual first when he and the brothers in Cuyahoga Lodge no. 95 of the Elks produced a circus to raise money for a new facility. In January 1924, the *Cleveland Gazette* announced,

Arrangements have been started for the production of a big indoor circus by the local lodge of Improved Benevolent and Protective Order of Elks of the World. It is to be a regular circus with animals both wild and tame, acrobats, aerialists, clowns and everything that is usually found with the outdoor shows and it will be the first affair of its kind ever sponsored by organizations or our race. . . . The entertainment will be a regular three-ring circus of the type that are seen in the summer time under the big tents. The committee in charge promise[s] a REAL show, with every feature of the big outdoor entertainments. [The Knisely Brothers Circus] has been engaged to produce the show and have contracted to present the same show as used by them during the summer.

Even before the *Gazette*'s official announcement, word of this undertaking had already begun to circulate among Cleveland's black and perhaps further, as the newspaper also reported that the venue had been changed from Gray's Armory to the larger Judd Auditorium to accommodate the anticipated crowds.[106]

Later in January, the *Gazette* revealed further details about this unusual promotion and the men who were spearheading it:

Through the wide acquaintance in the show world of P. G. Lowery and Sidney B. Thompson, chairman of the executive committee, some really very high class acts have been secured for the big indoor Elks' circus to be held in Judd Auditorium, the week of Feb 4th to 9th, inc., which include the famous "Riding Rooneys" who have for the past several years been the feature act of the Ringling Brothers' Barnum-Bailey circus. Among others are the Five Flying Fishers. . . . Ten clowns will produce laughs throughout the performance. One, "Baby Gene," only 19 months old, was the feature laugh-producer with the "Knisely Brothers Circus," the past season.

Lowery's name also appeared prominently in newspaper reports regarding the musical portion of the program: "Arrangements have been made for the famous Cleveland [Elks'] Band to furnish all music necessary for the circus, which will consist of 25 big acts. This band, under the direction of P. G. Lowery and Reuben Warren, has among its members many musicians from big summer circuses and shows."[107]

The out-of-season circus production caught public attention. For six days, the Elks may even have upstaged productions in such noted halls as Cleveland's Globe Theater. According to the *Gazette*, "The interest shown . . . is far exceeding the fondest hopes of the local committee, and by the time the doors are ready to open, Feb. 4th, they expect to have tickets in the hands of enough people to fill the house to capacity every night." Such hopes were realized, and the audience was pleased as well. Said the paper, "The Elks' circus is certainly packing them in, nightly, at Judd's great auditorium. It is really a wonderful show and thousands of our people are thoroughly enjoying it. It closes this Saturday night; so don't miss it whatever you do." Lowery's entertainment connections and the backing of the Elks had combined to produce a tremendously successful venture.[108]

THE FINALE OF
THE GOLDEN AGE

The 1931 Ringling Brothers season opened in New York, not in Madison Square Garden but on the golf links at the corner of Norstrand and Flatbush Avenues. The stand ran from May 18 through May 23. The sideshow manager was Clyde Ingall, who was credited with "embellishing" the exhibition. P. G. Lowery's Minstrel Company consisted of the band, orchestra, and comedians, some of whom also doubled as singers and dancers. The musicians included Lowery, director and cornet; Albert Kemp, assistant director and cornet; Willard Thompson, cornet; William Crable Jr. and Thomas Cook, trumpets; Howard Duffy and George E. Glenn, trombones; William Crable, mellophone; M. O. Russell, mellophone, saxophone, and orchestra leader; Walter Williams and C. A. Ivory, clarinets and saxophones; James L. Holmes and Edward W. Warren, percussions; Ben M. Goodall, euphonium; and William May, bass. The comedians were Charles Beechum, Rufus Dixon, Strawberry Russell, and Roland Canada.[1]

This circus season was very short and marked the beginning of ten years of calamities for traveling shows, with disasters running the gamut from bankruptcies to unionization to fires. The number of railroad shows and truck or motorized shows decreased. The golden age of the circus seemed to be winding down. The Cole Brothers show, reorganized by Zack Terrell and Jess Adkins, became the major competitor of the Ringling Brothers. Although other circuses remained on the scene—the Russell Brothers, the Downie Brothers, the Robbins Brothers, the Gorman Brothers, and Charlie Sparks—the Cole Brothers furnished the only real competition for the Ringlings.

This 1931 season was Lowery's final tour with the Ringling combine. Reminiscing more than ten years later, he gave no definitive reasons for leaving the show but stated simply, "April 16, 1919, joined the Ringling Brothers Circus, remained with them until September 12, 1931."[2]

According to his account, Lowery next conducted a concert band in the 1933 Chicago World's Fair and then joined the Gorman Brothers Circus on April 25, 1934. During this time, the seeds may have been sown for Lowery's involvement in a new circus that would challenge the Ringlings. At the Chicago World's Fair, Terrell managed a small, one-ring free circus that was operated by the Standard Oil Company. He would have had the opportunity to hear Lowery perform at the fair.[3]

Lowery subsequently connected with the Cole Brothers–Clyde Beatty Circus on April 4, 1935. Two men who had managed circuses for other people, Adkins and Terrell, organized this new circus in Rochester, Indiana, and

on April 20, 1935, a brand new major railroad circus opened in the Chicago Coliseum. The organization and building of this 35 car show by the late Jess Adkins and Zack Terrell from the ground up in a period of a few months was a miracle of management genius never surpassed in the annals of circus history. These two showmen took an idea and transformed it into reality in only six months. With their new Cole Brothers Circus they broke the monopoly the Ringling interests had held on railroad circuses and became the first show on rails to tour since 1931 that wasn't under the Ringling banner.[4]

On May 4, 1935, *Billboard* indicated that the executive staff and rosters of the various departments included another valuable item from the Ringlings' Show—Lowery's sideshow band. To be sure that Lowery and his entourage received the posh treatment to which they were accustomed, Lou Delmore, the sideshow manager, purchased a thousand dollars worth of velvet to be used as stage covers, draperies, and other white-top accoutrements.[5]

Lowery's skill with individuals and groups stood out as much as did his musicianship. This ability to deal with people was a major asset in his little-known secondary job with the circus, which involved handling route cards. Many circuses and other shows circulated these route cards, which enabled fans to follow the shows' travels and to plan to attend performances. Each show designated certain people to ensure the regular mailing of these cards to subscribers, and Lowery had this responsibility for the Cole Brothers Show. As part of his job, he would often inscribe personal messages on cards addressed to people whose names he recognized as regular patrons. As circus historian Tom Parkinson recalled,

Every week we would get a route card from him, and he would have some little note on it—maybe just "Hello!"—and then we would know where the show was. At every opportunity, we would go to that show, and he would be on the show grounds, oh, probably by noon, and we would look for him and then we would visit with him. I don't have an awful lot of recollections about what we talked about: it would be about how the show was doing and what they did in Indianapolis and things like that.[6]

By 1936, the Cole-Beatty sideshow was a strong contender against other shows and outdid the previous year's attendance records. And on April 17, 1937, the Cole Brothers–Clyde Beatty Circus opened its third season in front of a crowd of as many as twelve thousand people at Chicago Stadium. The circus's 1937–38 route book indicated that Lowery was the leader of the sideshow band, with an entourage that included Columbus Barefield, Jessie Barefield, Albert Bell, J. Browne, Nellie Browne, Claude Dickinson, Sammie Franks, Ben Goodall, Virginia Hartley, William Matthews, William May, and William Taylor.[7]

At the end of this tour, the Cole Brothers Circus route book proudly declared, "With its name emblazoned in gold from one end of spangleland to the other, the Cole Brothers Circus, America's greatest amusement institution, has just completed its third triumphal tour of the Continent." Furthermore, the book declared, the Cole Brothers Circus

travels 20,000 miles in a summer,
Exhibits more than 800 jungle animals in its colossal menagerie,
Carries over 1,000 people on tour, all of whom are given three meals each
day in the circus dining tents.
Daily expenses of show $7,500,
300 draft horses [are] carried to move the show,
250 ring stock horses in performance,
2,200 stakes driven and pulled each day,
[it] is the largest circus transported by rail that gives a street parade,
[and carries] More than 1,000 men, women, horses, elephants, camels,
yaks and other strange animals.8

Adkins and Terrell's successes had been great during the 1936 and '37 seasons, but conflicts began to develop between the two owner-partners, perhaps as a result of the two men acting as equals within the show. Adkins and Terrell had originally planned to have two shows, but that scheme fell through. In 1938, however, they decided that it was time to divide, with Adkins taking the fifteen-car Robbins Brothers Circus while Terrell assumed control of the Cole Brothers Circus.[9]

On April 30, 1938, Lowery opened with this new Robbins Brothers Circus, which had Milt Robbins as the manager of the sideshow. Lowery's band consisted of William Matthews, Sammy Frank, Wilbert Fields, William May, Ben Goodall, Hambone Williams, Billy and Marion Cornell, and Alma Williams—a mixture of performers who had previously worked with Lowery and newcomers.[10]

The 1938 summer season proved to be a difficult one for many shows, which were plagued by "bum business and at times bad weather." According to one account, "The Ringling Barnum show closed and returned to Sarasota in mid season. The . . . Downie shows closed early and the Cole show had its problems early in the season. The owners felt that [Cole Brothers] business would improve, but the show closed in Bloomington, Illinois on August 3rd." In the midst of all this failure, the Robbins show did relatively well, and some acts that had been with the Cole Brothers moved over to the Robbins outfit, which then headed south and had a successful remainder of the season.[11]

The next season, 1939, would not be prosperous for many shows. Perhaps in a defensive measure, Adkins and Terrell again joined together with a twenty-car Cole Brothers Show. But Lowery was not with them, having instead signed on with the Downie Brothers Circus. The Downie show opened in Macon, Georgia, on April 8 with a "variety of novel features, skillfully blended . . . with performances that won acclaim." Lowery's troupe consisted of twelve performers and worked under sideshow manager Milt Robbins, the former head of the Robbins Brothers sideshow. Unlike the other shows, which traveled by rail, the Downie Brothers had a "motor show" that traveled in a convoy of trucks.[12]

Some observers perceived Lowery's move to the Downie Brothers Show as a step down. And although the show was different, levels of tumult remained much like those he had endured in previous seasons. After opening in Macon, Georgia, the Downie Brothers Circus moved on to Thomaston and Griffin, Georgia; headed north, playing Chattanooga and five other Tennessee cities; and then traveled into West Virginia, Virginia, Ohio, and Pennsylvania. But as of the first week in May, the show had recorded only three profitable days since leaving Macon. Other problems then began to dog the show. At Steubenville, Ohio, the show site was switched at the last minute to a city-owned lot that was too small for the circus. At Warren, Ohio, cold weather resulted in a half-filled house for the main night show and in diminished sideshow business, even with Lowery as an attraction. Also at Warren, the billposters' union marked the Downie Brothers' posters "unfair" because the show had not signed an agreement with the Billers Alliance Union.[13]

The show then moved into the New England states, doing "fairly good business" in Waterville, Maine. The Downie Brothers' next stands were in New Jersey, where the show played before somewhat better houses, sometimes approaching capacity. Annapolis, Maryland, and Lynchburg, Virginia, followed. More misfortune struck in Lynchburg: a bad storm tore up the big-top canvas, which had to be replaced immediately. There was a sellout house at Norfolk, Virginia, but the Downie Brothers Show was now playing in close quarters with the Russell Brothers, Cole Brothers, and Parker and Watts Shows. Although the Cole Brothers Circus closed and did not meet some of its commitments in that area, patrons had been swamped by having so many different circuses visiting the area.[14]

While en route from Elizabethtown, Kentucky, to Nashville, Tennessee, in early September, the performers heard the news that Germany and Russia had invaded Poland and that England and France had declared war on Germany. In addition to all of the show's other problems, it now had to contend with the uncertainties associated with an emerging world war. Nonetheless, the Downie outfit doggedly moving on into Alabama, Mississippi, Louisiana, and Texas, but misfortune, including adverse weather and muddy lots, seemed to follow them. In Fort Worth, a record October heat wave negatively affected the matinee. The show seemed to sell just enough tickets to keep operating.[15]

Leaving Texarkana, Texas, after the November 1 show, the circus moved into Arkansas, playing Camden, El Dorado, Pine Bluff, Hot Springs, and Little Rock. On November 7, however, the Downie Brothers' show abruptly closed. The show was "temporarily" stored in Little Rock, with some animals and equipment sent to Houston for a Shrine circus. Nonetheless, the Downie Circus sent out Christmas cards boasting, "We'll be back in 1940."[16]

By March 1940, however, it had become obvious that the Downie Brothers Circus would not be coming back any time in the near future. The show had gone into receivership, and on March 23, 1940, *Billboard* announced, "DOWNIE BROTHERS CIRCUS, including title, to be offered for sale in immediate future. Inventory of assets and other information furnished on request."[17]

The Cole show was larger and had a somewhat more successful 1939 season, although the September 23 edition of *Billboard* reported that the drop in ticket sales as a result of the war had caused the Cole Brothers Circus to close and return to quarters. Yet another challenge arose as the show prepared for its 1940 opening: in early March, fire devastated the Cole Brothers' Rochester, Indiana, headquarters, killing animals, destroying equipment, and causing a total of $150,000 worth of damage. Despite the disaster, Terrell and Adkins vowed, "The show will go on."[18]

Friends and competing shows chipped in to lend equipment and other necessities to the Cole Brothers show. After the financial downturns of the 1939 season, only two railroad shows remained standing: the Ringling Brothers and Barnum and Bailey "Greatest Show on Earth" and the Cole

Brothers "Miracle Show." According to historian Joseph T. Bradbury, "Zack Terrell took off shortly after the fire to visit John R[ingling] North in Sarasota[, Florida,] and see what could be worked out in replacing some of the equipment and animals from the Ringling surplus in Peru[, Indiana]. His mission was successful and he was able to purchase [some equipment]." However, this assistance came with strings attached: the Cole Show had to agree not to perform in certain Midwestern cities and towns that the Ringlings coveted. Despite these restrictions, and in part because Adkins and Terrell "had very little equity in the property destroyed, still being in dire financial distress due to the recent bankruptcy and rather lean 1939 season," the Cole Show opened the 1940 season "as originally planned, but not without the greatest of difficulty in readying the circus for the road."[19]

None of the Cole Show's railroad cars had been badly damaged, so travel remained possible, but Adkins and Terrell decided to cancel street parades because they had lost so much specialized parade equipment. Lou Delmore managed the sideshow and had a fascinating array of attractions, including a Hawaiian review, a snake charmer, Siamese twins, and a sword swallower. P. G. Lowery's Band and Minstrels completed the lineup.[20]

People were becoming more likely to spend money for entertainment as they moved further away from the Great Depression of a decade ago, and the show did well during the 1940 season. Although Adkins died quite suddenly during the tour, Terrell and the managers who worked with him kept the circus running smoothly. The demand for entertainment was high, particularly in locales that offered war-related employment. In contrast to the preceding two years, Terrell was able to state that "our season . . . has been splendid. All our people are happy and satisfied. Workingmen will not only be paid in full but will also receive a bonus." At the end of the season, the show went to its new winter quarters in Louisville, Kentucky.[21]

The 1941 season picked up where 1940 ended. Terrell had overseen repairs, replacements, and other maintenance work, including a redesigned entrance and modernized lighting for the sideshow. On April 5, *Billboard* issued the call for "all performers, musicians, and sideshow people contracted with the [Cole Brothers] circus." The season would open on April 25 in Louisville.[22]

Arthur Windecker had become manager of the sideshow, and his collection of performers and oddities included exhibitions by former boxing champion Jack Dempsey, Siamese twins, monster reptiles, a magician, an "indestructible" girl, and P. G. Lowery and his thirteen Georgia Minstrels. In August 1941, Lowery wrote that "Jack Dempsey is proving a drawing card, and we are playing to big houses every day."[23]

The 1942 Cole Brothers season opened on April 22, the start of a five-day run in Louisville. After playing to good houses, the show moved on to Owensboro, Kentucky, Terrell's hometown. The sideshow attractions, "in addition to P. G. Lowery's Band and Minstrels, included freaks, novelty acts, and other features." Lowery's roster included Harvey Lankford, assistant leader; H. F. Chandler, saxophone; Billy Cornell, stage manager; Noah Robinson, comic and drummer; Walter G. Howell, cornet; Ben Goodall, baritone; William May, tuba; Charles Smith, trombone; Joe Jackson, clarinet; Oscar Jones; C. Hareld; and Alberta Snowden, Catherine Harold, Juanita Maniz, and Marion Cornell, chorus.[24]

By late August 1942, the Cole Brothers Circus was moving westward and doing good and steady business. In Salt Lake City, "where 90,000 imported war workers have been entertainment hungry for months," the show "hit the jackpot."

Despite 96 degrees and a sweltering sun, the matinee opened big. It was necessary to hold two shows at night, second beginning after 10 P.M., with aftershow lasting until early hours of the morning.

Head Press Agent Ora O. Parks arranged a one-hour radio show over station KLS. Col. Harry Thomas emceed the show which featured Victor Robbins' [big-top] Band [and] P. G. Lowery and his side show minstrel band. . . . Radio officials said it was one of the biggest radio shows featuring circus stars that had ever been produced over the airways.[25]

But more than fifty years of trouping had taken its toll on Lowery, who was now past seventy. Terrell had with difficulty persuaded Lowery to go home midway through the 1941 season, and some other unexplained gaps in his career may have resulted from illness. According to Parkinson, by the early 1940s, "P. G. was in poor health and his weekly letters told of his ailings. Early in the spring he blamed his troubles on the rains, later the

heat, and finally the cold. When the show was in the west, he explained
that the altitude bothered him. He would never recognize that the effect of
almost a half-century of constant moving was beginning to tell on him."
Lowery was hospitalized in Casper, Wyoming, during the Cole Show's
stand there in the fall of 1942. At the end of the season, Lowery went home
to Cleveland, and he died there on December 15, 1942. Said the *Eureka
Herald*, "He will be remembered by many."[26]

LOWERY'S LEGACY

During his lifetime, P. G. Lowery became a household name. He wrote edu-
cational articles, performed for presidents, critiqued musicians, and served
as the chief executive officer of a highly successful business enterprise.
Outstanding musicians, circus historians, and bandleaders, both black and
white, openly praised Lowery's work and contributions to the show life.
According to historian Sverre O. Braathen, for example, "Without any question of a doubt the greatest side show band director of all time was P. G.
Lowery, an excellent cornet player who could sting the high ones long and
loud as well as play all the best of the cornet solos when he had his own
minstrel show on the road. He directed bands on such leading circuses as
Ringling Brothers World's Greatest Shows; Ringling Barnum Robbins
Brothers, and Forepaugh Sells Brothers. He was also a composer. . . . Mr.
Lowery was a kindly, considerate person and gentleman in every sense of
the word and a very interesting conversationalist." Circus historian Bert J.
Chipman stated that "Much credit is due the Negro race for their contribution toward the success of the tented shows, and to no particular individual
more than . . . P. G. Lowery." Arthur L. Prince, Lowery's former stage manager, said that Lowery was a consummate musician, cornet virtuoso, and
[an] extremely kind man. He was always patient with his players, extending
a smile at the right moment. He was always satisfied to work quietly, allow-
ing others to enjoy praise. Prince said, "Spiritualists have said: 'His prosperity
is anointed with the blessings of the Almighty.'" H. Qualli Clark, a successful
bandleader whose career began as a cornetist with Lowery's bands, wrote and
dedicated a band composition, "Pee Gee's Blues," in Lowery's honor.[27]

As Lowery approached the end of his life and stellar career, his many friends began to ascribe increased meaning to his communications and to visits with him. His brief inscriptions on route cards left a lasting impression on Tom Parkinson and probably on many others in the circus audience. More than fifty years later, Parkinson fondly recalled his last meeting with Lowery, which took place around 1940:

> He was ill then I guess. I've often thought that circus people living on a train—the train would come in and the people would get off and put the circus together, and do the performances and all that—somebody that was ill would be on his own, just kind of deserted on that lonesome train. I've always thought of that as kind of a dismal way to be, particularly with bad weather as it was. That scene comes to mind when I think of him.
>
> But he was such a nice man, just so soft-spoken and friendly. He really gave you the notion that he was really delighted to see you turn up. He would be watching for [my brother] Bob and me as the show unloaded in Decatur. Or we also went to other towns, Peoria and Bloomington, to catch up with him.[28]

In addition to connecting with fans, Lowery not only built and maintained his own amazing career but also aided the professional development of many performers. Through what the *Indianapolis Freeman* termed the "Big Music School," Lowery unselfishly shared the musical knowledge that he had gained both on the road and at the Boston Conservatory.[29] Lowery also provided instruction to the numerous performers he employed in his road shows, and the artists who performed with Lowery early in their careers include Wilbur Sweatman, William "Bunk" Johnson, James Taylor, Charles Creath, Jeff Smith, J. J. Smith, Tom Tolliver, George Williams, Dan Desdunes, and singers Callie Vassar and Hattie Garland.

Lowery also indirectly influenced local musicians in Knoxville as well as other towns throughout the route card. Many aspiring musicians sought to emulate well-known performers. Knoxville's own real "Professor" was St. Clair Cobb. Booker wrote, "St. Cair Cobb was the [Black] community's band master for more than fifty years. He organized the first band at Knoxville College in 1936, and taught band at Austin High School. His bands performed at parades and conventions throughout the country."[30]

For many people, Lowery's life and career demonstrated that blacks could achieve success in the entertainment world with dignity and professionalism as long as one was highly skilled and wise in the ways of show business. Lowery set an unquestionable standard for quality in vaudeville, minstrelsy, and the sideshow.

THE AFTERSHOW

The Lowerys were not the only blacks to homestead on Spring Creek.
In the fifty years following the Civil War, sixteen black families had
settled in Spring Creek Township. Among those families associated
with this settlement were the Wrights, Greens, McCulloughs,
Stepters, Dukes, and Cracrafts. . . .
In the early days, the Lowery family established on their homestead [a]
small cemetery. . . . It would serve the African-American community
for many years. No record exists to tell us who is buried, . . . but many
believe that there are as many as thirty people, including several
members of the Lowery family.

—"DEDICATION CEREMONY, LOWERY CEMETERY AND
HOMESTEAD MEMORIAL MARKER, JULY 5, 1997"

Jeff Hokanson of the Greenwood County Historical Society Museum circulated small packets of information concerning the events for the July 4, 1997, weekend. The yellow sheet in the packet contained a map that indicated that we were at a site between Eureka and the Reece Township in Greenwood County. The ride from Eureka had taken about fifteen minutes. The view—farmland, pastureland, fencerows, and escarpments—was breathtakingly beautiful. Nature had presented one of

130

its best performances in this history-laden place. Looking farther to the southwest, one could see the boundary that at one time had divided the United States of America from the Indian territories. This might have been a trail that the Native Americans used to travel toward what became Eureka.

Henry Francis's roomy sedan slowly approached a group of perhaps thirty people standing in the middle of a well-defined dirt road. Henry was a former mayor of Eureka. Our arrival elicited smiles and greetings from those in the group who recognized us. Several were members of the historical society. Welcoming nods came from others who viewed us only as visitors or newcomers to the area. Since it was about 8:15, a bit of a chill remained in the morning air. The relatively brisk breeze caused some to huddle closely and tug at the sleeves of their garments. This breeze—wind, to us easterners—was blowing from the south over an area called Duke Hill, part of what had once been the Duke farm. The late I. N. "Nye" Duke was the last representative of the original families of color who settled the area during the land rushes of the 1870s. Many of the people present had known Nye personally.

On the shoulder of the road, four or so feet above the grade, was a gravestone marking the resting place of Thomas Cracraft, a Civil War veteran and one of the area's early African-American settlers. In front of the stone were two other items, a bouquet of faded blue plastic flowers and a tattered American flag. Someone had remembered to honor Cracraft. A larger item covered entirely in black plastic stood to the left of the Cracraft stone. Just across the barbed wire fence that marked the perimeter of the old Lowery farm were a few random footstones and other remnants of grave markers—the Lowery family cemetery.

Rev. Dan Wilson, minister of the Eureka Christian and Congregational Church, and the historical society's Bob Honeyman took their positions on the shoulder adjacent to the black-draped item. The attendees gradually ceased their conversations and drew closer to the roadside site. The yellow paper reminded me of the special events scheduled for this weekend—a quilt show in Eureka, a horse race at the Eureka Downs, a barbecue, and a Fourth of July parade. Yesterday, we had gone out into the vast Kansas countryside to visit Hap Jackson and his wife at their Flying J Ranch. Hap, a cowboy, rode the range with P. G.'s nephew, Gene Lowery. Although infirmity had caused Jackson to trade his horse for a wheelchair and had slowed his speech, he remained a wonderfully proud man. With the help of his wife, he shared photographs with us and told us many stories about the Lowery family. He inquired about our red, white, and blue caps bearing the legend "P. G. Lowery's Star of the West Brass Band." We gladly explained their significance. The next day, Hap rode in the parade in a large Cadillac sedan bearing a sign that read, "Hap Jackson, Friend of the Lowerys," testament to the family connections that remained in the area. He proudly wore one of our hats.

Earlier on the previous morning, the Reverend Lynn Siefert and I had journeyed to a house trailer, bristling with antennas and sitting atop a hill on the outskirts of Eureka—the local radio station. Siefert interviewed me for his community-interest show, and listeners perhaps learned a little more about their community's history. In his following Sunday sermon, Siefert would highlight the work ethics of the Lowerys and the other black settlers. We invited the listeners to join us at the roadside ceremony to be held the following day.

With Rev. Wilson's invocation now concluded, Honeyman recognized several people whose contributions and efforts had brought about this observance. The trusty yellow sheet reminded me that after this event would come at least two others of significance, a program presented by the Kansas Cowboy Poets and a ranch rodeo. This was indeed cowboy territory.

Bob Hodge, a member of the historical society, was standing near the black-draped item and began to address the group.

The members and friends of the Greenwood County Historical Society are devoted to seeking out information about people who have lived, and the events that have occurred, within the boundaries of the county since its establishment in 1855.

They are devoted to recording, preserving and disseminating this information to all, within and beyond the county boundaries—proud of the successes and contributions the citizens have made; sometimes ashamed of, but not hiding or covering up, the failures.

Sometimes it takes an "outsider" to make us aware of what we have overlooked. When that happens, we take steps to correct our omissions. This is one reason we are here today.[1]

Somehow, the mood of this occasion seemed much more than an effort to apologize for an oversight, and as guests we felt more like adopted citizens of the area than outsiders. This occasion seemed to be a celebration not only of the Lowerys but also of a unique, hardy spirit that would drive people to accomplishment, even in the face of disobliging odds. These wonderful people knew no strangers, and their warmth surely reflected the gift of hospitality attributed to the Lowerys. Perhaps the outsiders had done nothing more than stimulate the ongoing work of the historical society and the curiosity of the citizens.

While Hodge's scholarly presentation continued, holding the crowd's attention, the breeze became a bit warmer and the solemnity of the occasion more evident.

A year ago, Dr. Watkins was brought to this spot—at that time unmarked except for the [Cracraft] stone. He was shown this pasture site and told it was the Lowery Cemetery, but its location was known only because of the memory of older residents and the marks on the county maps. There were no engraved stones—only some fieldstones marking the location of the graves just on the other side of the fence.

One challenge to the Society members is to research and record "who" is here. Could the grave of Perry Lowery be here? Some once said "yes," but today we say "probably not," although his final resting spot is still unknown.[2]

As the ceremony progressed, my mind traveled to another burial ground nearly a thousand miles away, perhaps the complete antithesis of the Greenwood County setting. Harvard Grove Cemetery stands as a quiet island on Cleveland's bustling east side.

I return to the here and now and realize that Bob Hodge is finishing his dedication. The representatives of the historical society make their proclamations, and various impromptu responses follow. Quiet reigns as the black wrapping is removed.

During that brief interval, I contemplate how the circus big top, the midway, and its white-top annexes have now become items of history, replaced by gigantic, impersonal civic auditoriums. The sideshow bands are no more, and the big-top musicians in most shows are esoteric electronics without need for any real windjammers. As a result of many misrepresentations, some people now perceive the traveling minstrel shows as reflecting only negative elements of society. Within African-American society, these shows remain culturally and historically suspect. Perhaps the only contemporary cultural link to the old sideshows—the minstrels, the one-wagon medicine shows, the vaudeville entertainers, whether on rails or trucks—is Cal Dupree and Cedric Walker's all-black UniverSoul Circus, which is based in Atlanta and "claims to be the world's only African-American-owned circus, [bringing] a flavor steeped in black aesthetics and culture."[3]

Monuments occasionally appear in unexpected but unique places. A Philadelphia doll museum prominently displays a P. G. Lowery likeness wearing a neatly replicated Ringling Brothers sideshow band uniform. The porcelain doll was created by Chicago doll artist Roberta Bell as part of her Black Heritage Series collection, which included Harritt Tubman, Dr. Charles Drew, and others. The year of its creation is unknown, and the artist and her spouse are now deceased. Her motivation to create the Lowery doll might have been rooted in a now unconfirmable familial relationship—both Bell and Lowery were originally from Topeka, Kansas.[4] A printed card provides "Notes on P. G. Lowery." According to Barbara A. Whiteman's catalog for the exhibit, "Dolls as artifacts of history and culture tell a story about their past. More than play toys, these dolls symbolize the struggle for freedom and human dignity."[5]

The unveiling is completed. Following a period of quiet appreciation, we all begin to applaud as we perceive that the cloaked object is a simple but majestic marker stone bearing the inscription *Lowery*. As Hodge said, "We mark this spot so that all who travel this road, or come searching, may know that this area of the county was 'home' to the Lowery family."[6]

Rev. Wilson begins to deliver the benediction, but my attention is diverted to a busy newspaper reporter, perhaps from the *Eureka Herald*. The presence of a reporter would be entirely appropriate since the *Herald* was Lowery's longtime friend. It represented the link with the Greenwood-Eureka community that remained so very proud of him and his accomplishments.

Just as Andrew Lowery proved out his homestead claim, his son P. G. proved out his claim as a professional musician and successful entrepreneur despite operating in a segregated society and in a segment of the entertainment industry that was ignored by New York's Broadway theatrical critics. His honest hard work resulted in genuine respect from his fellow human beings, both black and white.

Writing sometime after Lowery's death, circus historian Tom Parkinson offered a poignant eulogy for his friend:

Mud was ankle deep and rain beat on the sagging tents. I asked the sideshow spieler if P. G. Lowery was with the circus that season. The fellow smiled and tilted his head.

"I guess old P. G. will be with it as long as it is out," he answered. That is the life story of this old colored sideshow bandleader. A veteran trouper and a tradition in this business where long years of service are commonplace. But the spieler was wrong for that [1942] was the last season P. G.'s silver cornet was to lure circus-goers into the tent housing "freaks, wonders, curiosities, amazing attractions never seen before."

Here was a man who had seen great changes come to his little world of sawdust and spangles. For forty-three summers he had answered a sideshow manager's call of "Bally" with the music of his brass band, sometimes playing his own compositions. When he first joined the circus the big names in that field—Bailey, Ringling, Forepaugh, Wallace, Robinson—were fighting for supremacy. He saw John Ringling win out and buy every major circus in the country. When he began his career, horses did all of the work on a circus and during his last few season[s] he saw tractors replace them. He saw the first air conditioned tents, public-address systems, and mechanical stake drivers appear. And he saw old-time street parades dropped from the daily schedule.

He was a man of few interests. He loved the circus as it loved him, and his friends among show people and circus fans were legion. He was considered a musician worthy of more than the humble position he held. ... Even the winter months he spent in Cincinnati [sic] seemed years to him and he looked forward to that day in the spring when he would board a circus train, when once again he would play his battered cornet as snake charmers and sword swallowers performed.[7]

Another timbre now replaces that of the minister's resounding voice, a revisitation of the great sound from the Great Plains—the inimitable resonance of a trumpet bringing forth Paul Richards's rendition of "Taps." The moving tribute reaches each element of the environment. Listening closely, one can nearly perceive the sounds of two like instruments. The Showman is responding across the Great Plains of time.

EPILOGUE

It is 1999, two years after the dedication ceremony, and I am once again in two places at once. As I stand at the Lowery memorial in Greenwood County, Kansas, I also stand at the confirmed burial site of the World's Greatest Colored Cornet Soloist. This is section 24, row 18, grave 8, of the Harvard Grove Cemetery in Cleveland, an attractive, well-maintained site. No gravestone marks this spot as P. G. Lowery's ultimate resting place. There is also no indication that Carrie Gilbert Lowery was also buried here after her death on June 21, 1943, at age fifty-nine.

The Lowerys' deaths resulted in probate and taxation matters in both Kansas and Ohio. The records of these legal proceedings provide both insight and mystery. P. G. Lowery left no will. His wife inherited all his property. His legacy was a great deal of goodwill and a single known composition, "The Prince of Decorah Galop."

Carrie Gilbert Lowery's will left the Cleveland house where she and P. G. had lived, as well as the residence's furnishings, to her son, Arthur Sanders. At her death, Carrie also owned farmland in Greenwood County, Kansas, part of the original Andrew Lowery homestead, valued at $1,120, including the oil interests therein. She left this property to Elmer Curtis Underwood of Cleveland, and he ultimately sold the property. Virtually no information about Underwood has been found, and his connection to Carrie Lowery remains unknown.[1]

A bouquet of sunflowers, the Kansas state flower, and a small stone from the Flint Hills rest on the Lowery grave site in Cleveland, paying homage, in both locations, to the musician and philosopher who said, "Good things come to he who waiteth, so long as he hustleth while he waiteth."

May the goose hang high,
May the ghost walk reg'lar, and
May ev'ry day be a 4th of July
—CEW[2]

NOTES

1. THE FLINT HILLS SETTLERS

1. Painter, *Exodusters*, 108.
2. Painter, *Exodusters*, 146; Katz, *Black West*, 179.
3. Wood, *Kansas Beef Industry*, 4.
4. *Eureka Herald*, May 27, 1897; Lindamood, "African-American Families."
5. *Eureka Herald*, October 26, 1875.
6. Lindamood, "African-American Families."
7. *Eureka Herald*, December 20, 1877, November 9, 1882.
8. Dobler, "History," 41.
9. Lindamood, "African-American Families."
10. *History of Greenwood County*.
11. The Homestead Act of 1862 allowed every adult male to acquire 160 acres if he lived on the land for five years and made improvements valued at one hundred dollars each year (Faulk, *Land*). The Timber Culture Act of 1873 provided that settlers could obtain an additional 160 acres by planting 40 acres of trees (Faulk, *Land*, 235).
12. Andrew Lowery, Record Book No. 18, p. 121; Andrew Lowery, U.S. Patent, W 1/2 SW 1/4/ 22, 26, 9 & s of SE 1/4 21, 26, 9; "Lowery" (document), Greenwood County Historical Society, Eureka, Kans.
13. Kansas Census, 1875; *Eureka Democratic Messenger*, February 9, 1923; *Eureka Herald*, March 4, 1875.
14. "Lowery" (document), Greenwood County Historical Society, Eureka, Kans.
15. Dobler, "History," 30.
16. Ohio, Department of Health, death certificate for Perry G. Lowery, December 15, 1942, file no. 9493; data gleaned from various sources including U.S. and Kansas census information and letters from Historians at Greenwood County Historical Society.

139

17. *Eureka Herald*, December 2, 1880, March 9, 1882; Ohio, Department of Health, death certificate for Perry G. Lowery, December 15, 1942, file no. 9493; *Eureka Herald*, March 9, 1882.

18. *Eureka Herald*, August 19, 1875, October 6, 1899, November 16, 1933.

19. U.S. Census, 1870; *Eureka Herald*, April 30, 1886. For other early mentions of James, see *Eureka Herald*, April 25, 1878 and July 18, 1878.

20. *Indianapolis Freeman*, December 6, 1911; April 13, 1912; *Eureka Herald*, April 14, 1912.

21. U.S. Census, 1870; Kansas Census, 1885; *Eureka Herald*, August 7, 1884.

22. Gene Lowery obituary, *Eureka Democratic Messenger*, February 9, 1923. For a reference to Gene Lowery, see *Eureka Herald*, December 9, 1887. In 1997, Ray Davidson wrote a poem about Gene entitled "Cowboy Poet," unpublished.

23. U.S. Census, 1870; *Eureka Herald*, February 3, 1888.

24. U.S. Census, 1870, 1875, 1880; *Eureka Herald*, March 23, 1882.

25. *Eureka Herald*, January 17, 1878, December 8, 1921; *Indianapolis Freeman*, December 16, 1911. For references to a street fight involving the teenaged Jesse, see *Eureka Herald*, February 10, 1877.

26. *Eureka Herald*, February 5, 1897.

27. Carrie G. Lowery to Tom Parkinson, April 21, 1943, Parkinson Papers; U.S. Census, 1870; Bradford, "Perry Lowery," citing an article taken from *Eureka Herald*, July 23, 1931. There are some inconsistencies regarding the year of P. G. Lowery's birth: in a 1941–42 interview, Lowery gave his year of birth as 1871 ("A Sketch of P. G. Lowery's Life [His Own Words]," 1941–42, Kachel Papers); his death certificate says 1877 (Ohio, Department of Health, death certificate, file no. 71636). However, the 1870 census lists him as being eight-twelfths of a year old, which agrees with the date of birth his widow gave in letter she wrote to Tom Parkinson just two months before her death (Carrie G. Lowery to Tom Parkinson, April 21, 1943, Parkinson Papers).

28. "Sketch"; Seymour interview. Kachel quotes Lowery as saying that he had "entered the music school in Boston, May 22, 1887" ("Sketch"). The Boston Conservatory's building burned during the 1960s, destroying the records of Lowery's specific course of study. Perry's stepbrother, Ed Green, attended the New England Conservatory.

2. GOING ON THE ROAD

1. Fletcher, *One Hundred Years*, 59.

2. Anonymous source. Verifying the actual existence of red-lighting is difficult because admitting to the practice could leave a company liable in the event of injury to a performer. Enough stories have been circulated, however, that the practice probably existed.

3. Fletcher, *One Hundred Years*, 43.

4. Brooks, *America's Black Musical Heritage*, 177–78.

5. Southern, *Music*, 301; Brooks, *America's Black Musical Heritage*, 178.

6. Brooks, *America's Black Musical Heritage*, 179–80; Southern, *Music*, 303; Fletcher, *One Hundred Years*, 55. Although Cole did much to revitalize the stage performance, he also came under criticism for his choice of titles. Regardless of the defenders who maintained that it was not meant to be negative, the use of the term *coon* in reference to a group of people rapidly became an undesirable and unacceptable racist epithet. Sylvester Russell of the *Indianapolis Freeman* and other black writers of the time rallied against the use of that term, sensitizing their readers within and without the profession, until *coon* was forced into disuse (Jasen and Jones, *Spreadin' Rhythm Around*, 23–75).

7. Knox, *Slave and Freeman*, 31.

8. *Indianapolis Freeman*, March 14, 1899. The February 18, 1911, edition of the *Indianapolis Freeman* announced that copies could be purchased in London, England.

9. *Indianapolis Freeman*, December 2, 1886. *At liberty* meant currently unemployed but seriously looking for show work.

10. *Indianapolis Freeman*, October 1, 1904, July 3, 1909, December 14, 1912.

11. "A Rabbit's Foot Company Gives Bad Show." *Indianapolis Freeman*, July 3, 1909.

12. *Indianapolis Freeman*, February 12, 1910.

13. *Indianapolis Freeman*, January 29, 1910.

14. *Indianapolis Freeman*, January 29, 1910.

15. *Indianapolis Freeman*, November 20, 27, 1897.

16. *Eureka Herald*, June 11, 1897.

17. *Indianapolis Freeman*, November 13, 1897.

18. May, *Circus*, 122.

19. Durant, *Pictorial History*, 157.

20. Draper, "Thirty-nine Years," 13. Sweeney stayed with Wallace for twenty-five years as Jack of all professions–acrobat, clown, equestrian director, musician, and rider.

21. Draper, "Thirty-nine Years," 13.

22. *Eureka Herald*, January 14, 1909. Because the conservatory records were destroyed in a fire during the 1960s, details of Lowery's tenure there cannot be confirmed.

23. Bradford, "Perry Lowery"; *Eureka Herald*, May 1, 1896.

24. On December 7, 1889, the *Indianapolis Freeman* reported, "There are two companies of Nashville Students now on the road and both are traveling in the State of Missouri."

25. Seroff, "Gospel Arts Day," 4.

26. *Indianapolis Freeman*, December 18, 1897.

27. *Indianapolis Freeman*, November 30, 1901.

28. *Eureka Herald*, May 31, 1895.

29. *Eureka Herald*, July 19, 1895.

30. *Eureka Herald*, July 26, August 2, 1895.

31. *Eureka Herald*, August 9, 1895, February 14, 1896; *Indianapolis Freeman*, February 22, 1896.

32. *Eureka Herald*, October 4, 1895.

33. *Eureka Herald*, February 21, March 20, 1896.

34. *Eureka Herald*, March 27, 1896.

35. *Eureka Herald*, May 1, 8, June 19, 1896.

36. Roster gleaned from the *Indianapolis Freeman*, January 16, 23, 1897. A smaller group of instrumentalists extracted from the band, for certain performances, was called the orchestra. The "orchestra leader" and "band director" were often two different people. Dan Desdunes led orchestras and brass bands in Omaha, Nebraska, from 1916 until the early 1950s. In addition, he toured with minstrel troupes and vaudeville companies (Pearson, *Goin' to Kansas City*, 33; Southern, *Music*, 258).

37. *Eureka Herald*, October 2, November 29, December 4, 1896. No other information has been found concerning Lowery's association with the Jackson Band. Lowery may have simply been under contract to appear as a guest soloist, as he periodically did with various bands, and news of this guest performance may simply have been overstated.

38. *Eureka Herald*, February 26, March 5, 1897.

39. *Eureka Herald*, June 11, October 1, 1897.

40. *Eureka Herald*, December 17, 1897.

41. *Indianapolis Freeman*, February 5, 19, 1898.

42. *Indianapolis Freeman*, March 26, 1898; *Memphis Daily*, February 19, 1898; *Nashville Evening Journal*, February 1898.

43. *Indianapolis Freeman*, April 2, 1898.

44. *Eureka Herald*, July 1, 1898; *Indianapolis Freeman*, September 17, 24, 1898.

45. *Topeka Daily Capital*, June 1, 1898.

46. *Topeka Daily Capital*, June 1, 1898.

47. *Indianapolis Freeman*, September 3, 17, 1898. See also Collins, *Oh, Didn't He Ramble*, 49.

48. Montgomery, *William C. Handy*, 14.

49. *Indianapolis Freeman*, March 20, 1897; W. C. Handy, *Father*, 65.

50. W. C. Handy, *Father*, 66.

51. W. C. Handy, *Father*, 66.

52. W. C. Handy, *Father*, 66.

53. *Indianapolis Freeman*, November 5, 1898.

54. Information provided by Wayne Shirley, Library of Congress, Washington, D.C. The *Indianapolis Freeman*, November 26, 1898, referred to the same group of performers as J. E. George's Operatic Minstrels.

55. *Indianapolis Freeman*, November 12, 26, December 3, 1898.

56. Collins, *Oh, Didn't He Ramble*, 49.

57. *Indianapolis Freeman*, December 24, 1898.

58. *Indianapolis Freeman*, January 7, 1899.

59. *Indianapolis Freeman*, March 3, 1899.

60. *Indianapolis Freeman*, April 17, 1899. Trombonist Fountain B. Wood succeeded Lowery as director and conductor of the Georgia Up-to-Date.

61. *Indianapolis Freeman*, July 8, 1899.

62. *Indianapolis Freeman*, April 8, 1899.

63. *Indianapolis Freeman*, July 9, 1910.

64. *Indianapolis Freeman*, December 2, 1899. James Taylor subsequently appeared on a September 6, 1928, Victor recording of Bennie Moten's Kansas City Orchestra (Rust, *Jazz Records*). Coon songs, sometimes called coon shouts, were a popular form of the late nineteenth and early twentieth centuries. Some sources claim that the word came from the term "baracoon," a kind of prison or stockade. If so, these first songs were possibly like a pre-blues prison or work song. If this is the case, then the term is without racial overtones, although the songs' debasing and insulting lyrics became controversial, and the form eventually fell from popularity (*Indianapolis Freeman*, January 2, 1909).

65. *Indianapolis Freeman*, July 22, 1899.

66. *Indianapolis Freeman*, December 2, 1899.

67. *Indianapolis Freeman*, December 2, 1899.

68. *Indianapolis Freeman*, December 30, 1899.

69. *Indianapolis Freeman*, January 13, 1900.

70. *Eureka Herald*, February 23, 1900.

71. *Indianapolis Freeman*, May 5, 1900.

72. *Indianapolis Freeman*, May 5, 1900.

73. *Indianapolis Freeman*, June 2, 1900.

74. *Indianapolis Freeman,* July 21, 1900.

75. *Indianapolis Freeman,* August 18, 1900.

76. *Indianapolis Freeman,* November 10, 1900.

77. *Indianapolis Freeman,* November 10, 1900.

3. LOWERY'S PROGRESSIVE MUSICAL ENTERPRISE

1. *Eureka Herald,* January 14, 1901.

2. *Indianapolis Freeman,* June 22, 1901, et seq.

3. *Indianapolis Freeman,* September 6, 1902; Berlin, *King of Ragtime,* 109.

4. Berlin, *King of Ragtime,* 82, 102; *Indianapolis Freeman,* October 4, 18, 1902; *Circus Report,* March 4, 1996.

5. Curtis, *Dancing,* 113–17.

6. *Indianapolis Freeman,* April 26, 1902; Fletcher, *One Hundred Years,* 149. The Missouri-born Sweatman (1882–1961) was largely self-taught on both clarinet and violin. He traveled both with large circus bands and with Mahara's Minstrels and did not remain for long with Lowery but pursued a vaudeville career as a novelty clarinetist and orchestra leader. Sweatman "conducted theater orchestras in Chicago during the years 1910–13, then moved into the world of vaudeville." Sweatman's orchestras included such future stars as Jimmie Lunceford and Edward Kennedy "Duke" Ellington (Feather, *Encyclopedia,* 317, 434; Southern, *Music,* 351; Haskins, *Black Music,* 83).

7. *Indianapolis Freeman,* May 10, 1902.

8. *Indianapolis Freeman,* May 10, 1902.

9. *Indianapolis Freeman,* May 17, 1902.

10. Bradford, "Perry Lowery."

11. *Indianapolis Freeman,* March 24, 1900.

12. The *Indianapolis Freeman,* May 24, 31, 1902, first indicated that Lowery was sick and had missed several performances. *Indianapolis Freeman,* December 6, 1902.

13. *Indianapolis Freeman,* May 16, 1903. The show's name came Luella's two husbands, John Forepaugh (1852–95), nephew of Adam Forepaugh; and George F. Fish, a former advertising manager for the *Philadelphia Inquirer* ("Luella Forepaugh-Fish Wild West" file, Circus World Museum, Baraboo, Wisc.).

14. *Indianapolis Freeman,* August 1, 1903. This information, provided by Circus World Museum, is a copy of an anonymous newspaper clipping from Ashland, WI, June 28, 1903.

15. *Indianapolis Freeman,* August 15, 1903.

16. *Indianapolis Freeman,* August 1, 1903.

17. *Janesville (Wisconsin) Recorder and Times,* July 30, 1903.

18. *Janesville (Wisconsin) Recorder and Times,* July 30, August 6, 1903; *Indianapolis Freeman,* August 15, 1903.

19. *Indianapolis Freeman,* October 31, 1903, 83. Ellistine P. Holley, "Sam Lucas," stated that "Samuel Milady, more popularly known as Sam Lucas, was one of the important "pace-setting stars" in breaking new ground for black entertainers. His career as a minstrel star, song writer, and actor on the American stage spanned nearly a half century, and his performing activities included the major forms of 19th and early 20th century popular theater."

20. *Indianapolis Freeman,* November 7, 1903.

21. *Indianapolis Freeman,* November 7, 1903.

22. *Indianapolis Freeman*, November 14, 1903.

23. *Indianapolis Freeman*, October 1, 1903.

24. *Indianapolis Freeman*, November 21, 28, 1903.

25. *Indianapolis Freeman*, November 28, December 19, 1903.

26. *Indianapolis Freeman*, December 26, 1903.

27. *Eureka Herald*, February 2, 1904.

28. *Indianapolis Freeman*, February 27, 1904.

29. *Indianapolis Freeman*, December 24, 1904, and April 1, 8, February 4, 1905.

30. *Indianapolis Freeman*, April 23, May 7, 21, 28, June 4, 1904.

31. *Indianapolis Freeman*, July 9, 1904.

32. *Indianapolis Freeman*, November 26, 1904; "Sketch."

33. *Indianapolis Freeman*, July 16, November 26, 1904.

34. *Indianapolis Freeman*, December 24, 1904, February 18, March 18, 1905.

35. *Official Programme*.

36. *Indianapolis Freeman*, November 14, 1904, and February 4, March 18, April 8, 1905.

37. *Indianapolis Freeman*, April 1, 1905.

38. "Sketch." *Indianapolis Freeman*, June 3, 10, 17, 1905.

39. *Indianapolis Freeman*, June 10, 1905, July 15, 22, 1905. Elliott died the following December (*Indianapolis Freeman*, December 16, 1905).

40. *Indianapolis Freeman*, August 5, 1905.

41. *Indianapolis Freeman*, August 12, 1905.

42. *Indianapolis Freeman*, September 23, 30, 1905.

43. Bennett, "Circus Musicians," 24. Although the "Prince of Decorah Galop" is Lowery's only known band composition, it is extremely likely that other compositions either remain undiscovered or lost. Slim Monfort moved into the old Lowery house in Reece and told me before he died that the attic was full of "old music." Unaware of its possible historical and artistic significance, Monfort discarded it. *Indianapolis Freeman*, October 21, November 4, 1905, and January 27, 1906.

44. *Indianapolis Freeman*, May 5, 26, June 9, 1906.

45. *Indianapolis Freeman*, June 30, July 21, August 25, 1906.

46. *Indianapolis Freeman*, July 14, August 25, 1906.

47. *Indianapolis Freeman*, October 13, 1906.

48. *Indianapolis Freeman*, December 15, 1906.

49. *Indianapolis Freeman*, December 15, 1906.

50. *Indianapolis Freeman*, February 9, March 23, 1907.

51. *Indianapolis Freeman*, March 23, 1907.

52. *Indianapolis Freeman*, July 13, 1907.

53. *Indianapolis Freeman*, August 10, 1907.

54. *Indianapolis Freeman*, August 10, 1907.

55. *Indianapolis Freeman*, July 13, September 14, 1907.

56. *Indianapolis Freeman*, November 16, 30, December 28, 1907.

57. *Indianapolis Freeman*, December 28, 1907.

58. *Indianapolis Freeman*, February 29, 1908.

59. *Indianapolis Freeman*, April 4, 1908.

60. *Indianapolis Freeman*, April 18, May 16, 1908. Hattie Garland recorded blues for Gennett Records in 1927 (Goodrich, Dixon, and Rye, *Blues and Gospel Records*).

61. *Indianapolis Freeman*, August 1, October 24, 1908.

62. *Indianapolis Freeman*, October 31, 1908.

63. *Indianapolis Freeman*, October 17, 1908. Callie Vassar recorded blues for Gennett Records in 1923 (Goodrich, Dixon, and Rye, *Blues and Gospel Records*)

64. *Indianapolis Freeman*, November 28, 1908.

65. *Indianapolis Freeman*, December 5, 1908.

66. *Indianapolis Freeman*, January 30, February 20, 1909.

67. *Indianapolis Freeman*, May 8, 1909.

68. *Indianapolis Freeman*, May 8, 1909.

69. *Indianapolis Freeman*, May 8, 1909.

70. *Indianapolis Freeman*, July 9, 1909.

71. *Indianapolis Freeman*, July 24, 1909.

72. *Indianapolis Freeman*, July 17, August 28, 1909.

73. *Indianapolis Freeman*, September 11, 18, October 2, 9, 16, November 13, 1909.

74. *Indianapolis Freeman*, December 4, 25, 1909. For some reason, Lowery did not use the Nashville Students name during the 1909–10 season. The Nashville Students' operation may have been leased out to another production company, or Lowery and his business associates may have retired the title for reasons that are no longer readily apparent.

75. *Indianapolis Freeman*, December 4, 1909.

76. *Indianapolis Freeman*, March 12, 26, 1910.

77. *Indianapolis Freeman*, March 26, 1910.

78. *Indianapolis Freeman*, March 26, April 9, 1910.

79. *Indianapolis Freeman*, June 4, 1910.

80. *Indianapolis Freeman*, June 18, 1910.

81. *Indianapolis Freeman*, May 21, 1910. After the 1910 and 1911 seasons, the Forepaugh show was permanently retired.

82. *Indianapolis Freeman*, June 25, July 16, 1910.

83. *Indianapolis Freeman*, October 22, November 20, December 10, 1910.

84. *Indianapolis Freeman*, January 21, March 25, 1911.

85. *Indianapolis Freeman*, February 4, April 25, 1911.

86. *Indianapolis Freeman*, January 28, 1911.

87. *Indianapolis Freeman*, April 1, 1911; Doug Seroff to author, September 15, 1994.

88. *Indianapolis Freeman*, March 4, 25, 1911.

89. *Indianapolis Freeman*, April 15, 1911.

90. *Indianapolis Freeman*, May 6, 1911.

91. *Indianapolis Freeman*, May 6, 1911.

92. *Indianapolis Freeman*, July 1, 22, October 4, November 11, 1911. Lowery was one of very few performers of color who were professional endorsers of instruments.

93. *Indianapolis Freeman*, December 2, 16, 1911.

4. TO HIM WHO HUSTLES

1. Sobel, *Pictorial History*, 20–23; Caffin, "Vaudeville Music," 209.

2. DiMeglio, *Vaudeville*, 1.

3. Laurie, *Vaudeville*, 200–201.

4. *Indianapolis Freeman*, January 20, 1912.

5. *Billboard; Indianapolis Freeman*, March 16, 1912.

6. *Indianapolis Freeman*, January 27, 1912.

7. *Indianapolis Freeman*, December 23, 1911.

8. *Indianapolis Freeman*, January 6, 1912.

9. *Indianapolis Freeman*, February 17, 1912.

10. *Indianapolis Freeman*, February 12, 17, 1912.

11. *Indianapolis Freeman*, February 12, 1912.

12. *Indianapolis Freeman*, March 16, 1912.

13. *Indianapolis Freeman*, February 17, 1912.

14. *Indianapolis Freeman*, March 16, 1912.

15. *Indianapolis Freeman*, March 30, April 20, 1912.

16. *Indianapolis Freeman*, May 4, 1912.

17. *Indianapolis Freeman*, March 16, 1912.

18. *Indianapolis Freeman*, May 25, 1912.

19. *Indianapolis Freeman*, August 3, 24, 1912.

20. *Indianapolis Freeman*, February 12, November 9, 1912.

21. *Indianapolis Freeman*, August 10, September 28, 1912.

22. *Indianapolis Freeman*, August 24, 31, November 9, 23, December 14, 1912.

23. *Indianapolis Freeman*, December 14, 28, 1912.

25. *Indianapolis Freeman*, February 8, 1913.

24. *Indianapolis Freeman*, January 18, 25, 1913.

26. *Indianapolis Freeman*, January 25, February 8, 1913.

27. *Indianapolis Freeman*, April 12, 1913.

28. *Indianapolis Freeman*, April 12, 1913.

29. *Indianapolis Freeman*, March 15, 1913; Hagenbeck-Wallace Circus, *Route Book, 1913*.

30. Hagenbeck–Wallace Circus, *Route Book, 1913*.

31. *Indianapolis Freeman*, May 4, 31, June 14, 1913.

32. *Indianapolis Freeman*, May 31, 1913.

33. *Indianapolis Freeman*, May 31, June 8, 1913.

34. *Indianapolis Freeman*, June 14, 1913.

35. *Indianapolis Freeman*, June 28, August 30, 1913.

36. *Indianapolis Freeman*, August 30, 1913.

37. *Indianapolis Freeman*, October 4, 1913.

38. *Indianapolis Freeman*, September 6, October 11, 1913.

39. Hagenbeck–Wallace Circus, *Route Book, 1913; Indianapolis Freeman*, August 30, 1913.

40. *Indianapolis Freeman*, December 6, 1913.

41. *Indianapolis Freeman*, January 10, 1914.

42. *Indianapolis Freeman*, January 24, 1914.

43. *Indianapolis Freeman*, February 14, 1914.

44. *Indianapolis Freeman*, March 28, April 11, 1914.

45. *Indianapolis Freeman*, April 18, 1914.

46. Hagenbeck–Wallace Circus, *Route Book, 1914*.

47. Hagenbeck–Wallace Circus, *Route Book, 1914*.

48. *Indianapolis Freeman*, June 27, July 4, 1914.

49. *Indianapolis Freeman*, July 11, 18, 1914.

50. *Indianapolis Freeman*, September 12, 1914.

51. *Indianapolis Freeman*, October 17, 1914.

52. *Indianapolis Freeman*, January 16, 23, 1915.

53. *Indianapolis Freeman*, March 15, April 3, 1915.

54. *Indianapolis Freeman*, May 15, 22, 1915.

55. *Indianapolis Freeman*, June 5, 1915.

56. *Indianapolis Freeman*, June 12, 26, August 21, September 4, 1915.

57. *Indianapolis Freeman*, October 16, 1915.

58. *Indianapolis Freeman*, November 27, December 11, 1915, January 1, 1916.

59. *Indianapolis Freeman*, February 12, 1916.

60. *Indianapolis Freeman*, March 25, 1916.

61. *Indianapolis Freeman*, May 13, 20, June 10, 1916. Creath, later became a leading jazz trumpeter and contractor in St. Louis. Creath-led riverboat bands subsequently included such famous musicians as bassist Pops Foster, drummer Zutty Singleton, and singer-guitarist Lonnie Johnson. Creath later recorded for Okeh Records (Russell, *Jazz Style*, x, 71; Feather, *Encyclopedia*, 171.

62. *Billboard*, May 6, 1922. No date for the marriage has been found because the state of Ohio did not require marriage licenses until the 1950s.

63. *Indianapolis Freeman*, June 3, 24, July 8, August 12, 1916.

64. Danville Chamber of Commerce, Danville, Indiana, and Plainfield Police Department, Plainfield, Indiana.

65. *Indianapolis Freeman*, August 19, 1916.

66. *Indianapolis Freeman*, September 16, 1916.

67. *Indianapolis Freeman*, October 21, 1916.

68. *Indianapolis Freeman*, January 13, March 10, 24, 1917.

69. *Indianapolis Freeman*, May 5, 26, 1917.

70. *Indianapolis Freeman*, May 12, 1917.

71. *Indianapolis Freeman*, June 2, 16, July 7, 1917.

72. *Indianapolis Freeman*, July 14, 1917.

73. *Indianapolis Freeman*, September 1, 8, 1917.

74. *Indianapolis Freeman*, September 22, 1917.

75. *Indianapolis Freeman*, October 13, November 3, 1917.

76. *Indianapolis Freeman*, November 3, 14, 1917.

77. *Indianapolis Freeman*, November 24, December 8, 15, 22, 1917.

78. *Indianapolis Freeman*, January 5, 1918.

79. *Indianapolis Freeman*, January 12, 1918.

80. *Indianapolis Freeman*, February 9, 1918.

81. *Indianapolis Freeman*, March 23, April 20, 1918.

82. *Indianapolis Freeman*, May 4, 1918.

83. *Indianapolis Freeman*, May 11, June 1, 1918.

84. Indianapolis Freeman, June 22, July 13, 1918; Reeder, *No Performances Today*, 21, 142, back cover. Baker's minstrels were in a different section and thus were not directly involved in the disaster.

85. *Indianapolis Freeman*, September 7, 1918; Mayer, "Looking Back," 10; Chipman, *Hey Rube!* 123; Wintz, *Nitro*, 77. The "W. Johnson" listed as playing cornet may have been William Geary "Bunk" Johnson, a renowned New Orleans jazz trumpeter. Although Johnson claimed to have played with Lowery, some people who knew the trumpeter

alleged that his nickname "related to what came out of his mouth" and doubted his claim. However, Barry Kernfeld indicates that Johnson "worked outside New Orleans with McCabe's Minstrels and Hagenbeck's and Wallace's Circus Band before 1910. He appears to have left New Orleans finally around 1914 to travel with shows, joining P. G. Lowery's band in 1918" (*New Grove Dictionary*, 419). Christopher Hillman states that Johnson "probably spent a few years [between 1914 and 1918] touring with circus and minstrel shows. He claims to have worked in P. G. Loral's [*sic*] Circus, Holcamp's Georgia Smart Set, McCabes Minstrels and [the] Hagenbeck and Wallace's Circus. In Bunk's recollection all these activities took place during the first decade of the century. However one Willie, Bill, or W. Johnson turns up as a cornetist in press references to Baker's Concert Band of Nitro, West Virginia, in 1918. This band was led by P. G. Lowery, a well-known show band director and cornet virtuoso" (*Bunk Johnson*, 15, 36–37). A fire in the administrative area of the Nitro complex destroyed many of the personnel records relating to the World War I–era bands.

86. *Indianapolis Freeman*, September 28, 1918.

87. *Indianapolis Freeman*, December 21, 1918.

88. "Sketch"; Mayer, "Looking Back," 10. William "Shorty" Matthews was a much sought-after woodwind player who was one of Lowery's favorite musicians and who had a long tenure with the bandleader. Matthews kept a diary that describes the itinerant lifestyle typical of musicians of this era and shows the acceptability of a lifestyle in which professionals moved from job to job, returning to previous positions when necessary. Matthews's journal offers a remarkable overview of Lowery's professional endeavors in Cleveland and with the Ringlings beginning in March 1922 and continuing through 1938, when Lowery's group was part of the Robbins Brothers Circus, although Matthews did not play with Lowery continuously throughout this time.

89. Parkinson interview.

90. Parkinson interview.

91. *Billboard*, May 14, 1921; *Indianapolis Freeman*, August 2, 9, 16, 1919.

92. *Indianapolis Freeman*, September 13, 1919. Shortly before his visit to the farm, Lowery advertised for an "experienced farmer" to operate and manage his farm (*Indianapolis Freeman*, September 20, 1919).

93. *Indianapolis Freeman*, October 24, 1919.

94. *Indianapolis Freeman*, December 13, 1919.

95. *Indianapolis Freeman*, January 17, 1920. For some reason, Lowery subsequently ran a second ad asking musicians who responded to the January ad but received no reply to write again (*Indianapolis Freeman*, February 7, 1920).

96. Brown, "History," 197.

97. Brown, "History," 109; Davis, *Black Americans*, 213.

98. *Indianapolis Freeman*, February 7, 1920.

99. Southern, *Biographical Dictionary*, 250; *Cleveland Gazette*, April 1, 1922.

100. *Indianapolis Freeman*, March 20, April 17, 1920; Rehrig, *Heritage Encyclopedia*, 475; Fred Jewell, The *Indianapolis Star Magazine*, July 29, 1973, 9.

101. Lentz, "Merle Evans," 5.

102. *Indianapolis Freeman*, April 10, November 13, 1920.

103. *Indianapolis Freeman*, May 1, 8, 22, 1920. The May 8 piece marked the first time that Lowery's name was directly linked to the generic musical style known as jazz.

104. *Indianapolis Freeman*, November 13, 1920.

105. *Billboard*, March 19, 1921; Bob Pinsker to author, August 3, 2000. The Los Angeles review appeared in *Ragtime*, writer Billy Tucker's weekly newsletter about the city's black theatrical community, on September 23, 1922.

106. *Cleveland Gazette*, January 19, 1924.

107. *Cleveland Gazette*, January 19, 26, 1924.

108. *Cleveland Gazette*, January 26, February 9, 1924.

5. THE FINALE OF THE GOLDEN AGE

1. *Billboard*, May 23, 1931.

2. "Sketch."

3. "Sketch;" "History of the Cole Brothers Circus," *Bandwagon*, May–June 1965, 4–8.

4. Parkinson interview; Bradbury, "History," 4.

5. *Billboard*, May 4, 1935.

6. Parkinson interview.

7. *Billboard*, May 16, 1936; Bradbury, "History," 19; *Bandwagon*, March–April 1966, 18; Cole Brothers Circus, *Route Book*.

8. Cole Brothers Circus, *Route Book.*

9. Parkinson, "Circusdom's Historic Personage," 8.

10. *Bandwagon*, November–December 1966, 26.

11. Bradbury, "History, Part XI," 15; "Forty Years in the Center Ring," *Bandwagon* 9, July–August 1965.

12. *Billboard*, April 15, 1939.

13. *Bandwagon*, September–October 1976, 18–21.

14. *Bandwagon*, September–October 1976, 20.

15. *Bandwagon*, September–October 1976, 21.

16. *Bandwagon*, September–October 1976, 21.

17. Bradbury, "History, Part VI"; *Bandwagon*, September–October 1976, 22.

18. *Billboard*, September 23, 1939, March 2, 1940; "Sketch"; Bradbury, "History."

19. Bradbury, "History, Part VI," 19; *Bandwagon*, September–October 1976, 18–19.

20. *Bandwagon*, September–October 1976, 28.

21. *Bandwagon*, September–October 1976, 22.

22. *Billboard*, April 5, 1941; *Bandwagon*, November–December 1976, 24.

23. *Bandwagon*, November–December 1976, 28; P. G. Lowery to Thomas Parkinson, August 21, 1941, Parkinson Papers, Circus World Museum.

24. *Bandwagon*, July–August 1977, 17; *Billboard*, May 23, 1942; Cole Brothers Circus, *Official Route, Program, and Personnel for the Season of 1942.*

25. *Billboard*, August 22, 1942.

26. *Bandwagon*, July-August 1977, 17; Parkinson interview; undated, untitled monograph, Parkinson Papers; "Perry G. Lowery Dies," *Eureka Herald*, December 1942. Although the *Herald* obituary stated that "he returned from a trip abroad with a gold cornet presented to him when he appeared at the Royal Court in England" and Bradford, "Perry Lowery," repeats this claim, I could find no further information regarding this alleged performance. Although European tours were discussed (see chap. 4), I found no evidence that Lowery ever actually played overseas, and such a tour would have been big news and received extensive newspaper coverage, particularly in the *Freeman*.

27. Braathen, "Chords and Cues"; Chipman, *Hey Rube!* 123; *Indianapolis Freeman*, January 27, 1912. Clark, "Pee Gee Blues," Pace & Handy Music Company, New York, 1919.

28. Parkinson interview.

29. *Indianapolis Freeman*, January 27, 1912, March 15, 1913, May 31, 1913.

30. Robert J. Booker, *Two Hundred Years of Black Culture in Knoxville, Tennessee, 1791 to 1991*, 48.

6. THE AFTERSHOW

1. Hodge, "Challenges."

2. Hodge, "Challenges."

3. Cynthia Greenlee, "Entertainment–The UniverSoul Circus," http://www.africana.com/Daily Articles/index_20010725.htm.

4. Telephone interview with Whiteman, January 2, 2003.

5. Whiteman, "Treasury."

6. Hodge, "Challenges."

7. Undated, untitled monograph, Parkinson Papers.

EPILOGUE

1. I found only two passing references to Underwood, in the *Cleveland Gazette*, December 25, 1920, and December 8, 1923. In Greenwood County, he was regarded as a stranger.

2. Clifford E. Watkins, I, *Circus Benediction*, 1995.

BIBLIOGRAPHY

PRIMARY SOURCES

Clarence Kachel Papers. Circus World Museum, Baraboo, Wisc.
William "Shorty" Matthews. Diary. Philadelphia Mini Circus, Penn.
Tom Parkinson Papers. Circus World Museum, Baraboo, Wisc.

PERIODICALS

78 Quarterly
Billboard magazine
Cleveland (Ohio) Gazette
Eureka (Kansas) Democratic Messenger
Eureka (Kansas) Herald
Fanfare
Indianapolis Freeman
Janesville (Wisconsin) Recorder and Times
Topeka (Kansas) Daily Capital

SECONDARY SOURCES

Adero, Malaika, ed. *Up South: Stories, Studies, and Letters of African-American Migrations.* New York: New Press, 1993.
"Alumni Breakfast Honoring Bishop John Gregg, Ninth President of Wilberforce University. . . . and the Class of 1898" [program]. Wilberforce University National Alumni, Xenia, Ohio, June 11, 1947.
Barnum, P. T. *Barnum's Own Story: The Autobiography of P. T. Barnum.* Ed. Waldo R. Browne. Gloucester, Mass.: Peter Smith, 1972.

Berlin, Edward A. *King of Ragtime: Scott Joplin and His Era*. New York: Oxford University Press, 1994.

Bennett, Charles, Jr. "Circus Musicians Who Composed Music." *Little Circus Wagon* 34 (December 1970–January 1971).

Booker, Robert J. *Two Hundred Years of Black Culture in Knoxville, Tennessee, 1791 to 1991*. Virginia Beach, Va.: Donning, 1993

Bowman, Harry P. *A Sunday Run*. Booklet. Jeannette, Penn.: n.d.

Boyd, Levi. *The Story of the Second Largest Circus in the World*. Fairbury, N.B.: Levi Boyd, 1957.

Braathen, Sverre O. "Chords and Cues." *Bandwagon* Vol. 15 (September–October 1971).

———. "The Old Circus Band." *White Tops* 29 (July–August 1956).

———. *Here Comes the Circus! The Rise and Fall of the Circus Band*. Evanston, Ill.: Instrumentalist Company, 1958.

Bradbury, Joseph T. "Cole Brothers Circus, America's Favorite Railroad Show, Season of 1941." *Bandwagon* Vol. 20, no. 6 (November–December 1976): 24–35.

———. "Cole Brothers Circus, America's Favorite Railroad Show, Season of 1942." *Bandwagon* Vol. 21, no. 4 (July–August 1977): 12–24.

———. "A History of the Cole Brothers Circus, 1935–40." *Bandwagon* Vol. 9 (May–June 1965): 4–19.

———. "A History of the Cole Brothers Circus, 1935–40: Part II, the 1935 Season." *Bandwagon* Vol. 9, no. 4 (July–August, 1965): 9–19.

———. "A History of the Cole Brothers Circus, 1935–40: Part VI, the Winter of 1936–37. Building of the Great 40 Car 1937 Show." *Bandwagon* Vol. 10, no. 2 (March–April 1966): 12–21.

———. "A History of the Cole Brothers Circus, 1935–40: Part VI, the 1938 and 1939 Seasons." *Bandwagon* Vol. 20, no. 5 (September–October 1976): 11–25.

———. "A History of the Cole Brothers Circus, 1935–40: Part X, the 1938 Robbins Brothers Circus." *Bandwagon* Vol. 10, no. 6 (November–December 1966): 22–30.

———. "A History of the Cole Brothers Circus, 1935–40: Part XI, the 1938 Season." *Bandwagon* Vol. 11 (March–April 1967): 14–25.

———. "A History of the Cole Brothers Circus, 1935–40: Part XII, the 1939 Season." *Bandwagon* Vol. 11, no. 3 (May–June 1967): 17–29.

———. "A History of the Cole Brothers Circus, 1935–40: Part XIII." *Bandwagon* Vol. 11 (September–October 1967).

Bradford, Helen. "Perry Lowery." Unpublished document, Greenwood County Historical Society.

Brooks, Tilford. *America's Black Musical Heritage*. Englewood Cliffs, N.J.: Prentice-Hall, 1984.

Brown, George. "The History of the Negro in Cleveland from 1800 to 1900." Ph.D. diss., Western Reserve University, 1934.

Caffin, Caroline. "Vaudeville Music." In *American Vaudeville as Seen by Its Contemporaries*, ed. Charles W. Stein. New York: Knopf, 1984.

Chan, Sucheng, Henry Daniels Douglas, Mario Garcia, and Terry Wilson, eds. *Peoples of Color in the American West*. Lexington, Mass.: D. C. Heath, 1994.

Chipman, Bert J. *Hey Rube!* Ed. Harry B. Chipman. [Hollywood, Calif.: Hollywood Print Shop,] 1933.

Cole Brothers Circus. *1937–38 Route Book*. Rochester, Ind.: [Cole Brothers Circus, 1938].

————. *Official Route, Program, and Personnel for the Season of 1942.* Rochester, Ind: [Cole Bros. Circus, 1942].

Collins, Lee. *Oh, Didn't He Ramble: The Life Story of Lee Collins.* Urbana: University of Illinois Press, 1989.

Croft-Cooke, Rupert, ed. *The Circus Book.* London: Low, Marston, 1948.

Curtis, Susan. *Dancing to a Black Man's Tune: A Biography of Scott Joplin.* Columbia: University of Missouri Press, 1994.

Dahlinger, Fred, Jr. "The Triumphal March of Melody: 200 Years of Circus Music." Speech presented at the Windjammers Unlimited Banquet, Baraboo, Wisconsin, July 24, 1993; reprinted in *Circus Fanfare* 23 (October 20, 1993).

Davis, Russell H. *Black Americans in Cleveland.* Washington, D.C.: Associated Publishers, 1972.

"Dedication Ceremony, Lowery Cemetery and Homestead Memorial Marker, July 5, 1997" [program]. Greenwood County Historical Society, Eureka, Kans.

de Lerma, Dominique-René. *Black Music in Our Culture: Curricular Ideas on the Subjects, Materials, and Problems.* Kent, Ohio: Kent State University Press, 1970.

DiMeglio, John E. *Vaudeville U.S.A.* Bowling Green, Ohio: Bowling Green University Popular Press, 1973.

Disher, M. Willson. *Fairs, Circuses, and Music Halls.* London: Collins, 1942.

Dobler, Grace. "The History of Eureka, Kansas, 1957–1970." Unpublished document, Greenwood County Historical Society, Eureka, Kans., n.d.

Draper, John. "Thirty-nine Years of Trouping with Charles and Winnie Sweeney." *Bandwagon* 23 (September–October 1979).

Durant, John, and Alice Durant. *Pictorial History of the American Circus.* New York: Barnes, 1957.

Faulk, Odie B. *Land of Many Frontiers: A History of the American Southwest.* New York: Oxford University Press, 1968.

Feather, Leonard. *Encyclopedia of Jazz.* New York: Horizon Press, 1960.

Fletcher, Tom. *One Hundred Years of the Negro in Show Business.* 1954; reprint, New York: DaCapo, 1984.

Garcia-Barrio, Constance. "The Black Big Top." *American Legacy Magazine* 5 (fall 1999).

Gaunt, Mary. "The Circus—Another Entertainment." In *Opera Houses and Entertainment, Pre-1950.* Woman's Kansas Day Club, n.d.

Gilbert, Douglas. *American Vaudeville, Its Life and Times.* New York: McGraw-Hill, 1940.

Goodrich, John, Robert M. W. Dixon, and Howard Rye, comps. *Blues and Gospel Records, 1890–1943.* 4th ed. New York: Oxford University Press, 1997.

Green, Bill. *Old Time Kansas Shows and Circuses.* Wichita, Kans.: Bette Leonard Tent, Circus Fans of America, n.d. Greenwood County Historical Society. General county history. Eureka, Kans., n.d.

Hagenbeck-Wallace Circus. *Route Book, Season 1913.* Peru, Ind: Hagenbeck-Wallace Combined Shows, [1913].

Route Book, Season 1914. Peru, Ind: Hagenbeck-Wallace Combined Shows, [1914].

Handy, D. Antoinette. *Black Women in American Bands and Orchestras.* Metuchen, N.J.: Scarecrow, 1981.

Handy, W. C. *Father of the Blues.* Ed. Arna Bontemps. New York: Macmillan, 1941.

Haskins, James. *Black Music in America: A History through Its People.* New York: Harper Trophy, 1987.

Hillman, Christopher. *Bunk Johnson: His Life and Times.* New York: Universe Books, 1988.

The History of Greenwood County, Kansas. Wichita: Jostens, 1986.

Hitchcock, H. Wiley, and Stanley Sadie, eds. *The New Grove Dictionary of American Music.* New York: Grove's Dictionaries of Music, 1986.

Hodge, Robert A. "Challenges—Past, Present and Future." Speech presented at the dedication of the Lowery Marker, July 5, 1997, Greenwood County, Kans.

Hoh, LaVahn G., and William H. Rough. *Step Right Up! The Adventure of Circus in America.* White Hall, Va.: Betterway, 1990.

Holley, Ellistine P. "Sam Lucas, 1840–1916: A Bibliographic Study." In *Feel the Spirit, Studies in Nineteenth-Century Afro-American Music,* ed. George Keck and Sherrill B. Martin. New York: Greenwood, 1988.

Jasen, David A., and Gene Jones. *Spreadin' Rhythm Around: Black Popular Songwriters, 1880–1930.* New York: Schirmer, 1998.

Jensen, Dean. *The Biggest, the Smallest, the Longest, the Shortest: A Chronicle of the American Circus from Its Heartland.* Madison: Wisconsin House, 1975.

Jones, LeRoi [Amiri Baraka]. *Blues People: Negro Music in White America.* New York: Morrow, 1963.

Katz, William Loren. *The Black West.* 3d rev. and exp. ed. Seattle, Wash.: Open Hand, 1987.

Keck, George, and Sherrill V. Martin, eds. *Feel the Spirit: Studies in Nineteenth-Century Afro-American Music.* New York: Greenwood, 1988.

Kernfeld, Barry, ed. *The New Grove Dictionary of Jazz.* 2d ed. Vol. 2. London: Macmillan, 2002.

King, Orrin Copple. "Only Big Show Coming, Exalted in Aim …" *Bandwagon* (September–October 1994).

Knox, George L. *Slave and Freeman: The Autobiography of George L. Knox.* Ed. and intro. Willard B. Gatewood Jr. Lexington: University Press of Kentucky, 1979.

Laurie, Joe, Jr. *Vaudeville from the Honky-Tonks to the Palace.* New York: Holt, 1953.

Lentz, John. "Merle Evans, His Final Interview (1987)." *Bandwagon* Vol. 32 (January–February 1988): 21–23.

Lindamood, Zenith. "African-American Families in Greenwood County History." Unpublished document, Greenwood County Historical Society, n.d.

May, Earl Chapin. *The Circus from Rome to Ringling.* New York: Duffield and Green, 1932.

Mayer, Bob. "Looking Back." *Circus Fanfare* 8 (October 20, 1978).

———. "Side Show Bands." *Bannerline,* October 15, 1974.

McIntyre, Charshee L. *African and African-American Contributions to World Music.* Portland, Oreg.: Publication Services, Portland Public Schools.

Miller, John W. *Indiana Newspaper Bibliography.* Indianapolis: Indiana Historical Society, 1982.

Montgomery, Elizabeth Rider. *William C. Handy, Father of the Blues.* New York: Dell, 1968.

Morrish, Ray Sells. "Sells Brothers Circus." *American-German Review* 21 (June–July 1955).

Murray, Albert. *Stomping the Blues.* New York: Da Capo, 1976.

Oakley, Giles. *The Devil's Music: A History of the Blues.* New York: Taplinger, 1977.

Official Programme of Exercises and Illustrated History Commemorating the Inauguration of Theodore Roosevelt as President of the United States—Charles W. Fairbanks as Vice-President of the United States. Washington, D.C.: Otto A. Sontag, 1905.

Official Souvenir Program, Inaugural Ceremonies, March 4, 1901. Ed. and comp. by the Committee on Printing, Isadore Saks, Chairman. Washington, D.C., 1901.

Oliver, Paul. *Savannah Syncopators: African Retentions in the Blues*. New York: Stein and Day, 1970.

Olmstead, Andrea. "A History of the Boston Conservatory of Music." Unpublished document, June 1985. Boston Conservatory, Boston, Mass.

Painter, Nell Irvin. *Exodusters: Black Migration to Kansas after Reconstruction*. New York: Norton, 1979.

Parkinson, Thomas. "Circusdom's Historic Personage." *Bandwagon* Vol. 10, no. 3 (May–June 1966): 4–13.

Pearson, Nathan W., Jr. *Goin' to Kansas City*. Urbana: University of Illinois Press, 1987.

Plowden, Gene. *These Amazing Ringlings and Their Circus*. Caldwell, Idaho: Caxton, 1967.

Reeder, Warren A., Jr. *No Performances Today: June 22, 1918, Ivanhoe, Indiana*. [Hammond, Ind.: North State Press,] 1972.

Rehrig, William H. *The Heritage Encyclopedia of Band Music: Composers and Their Music*. Ed. Paul E. Bierly. 3 vols. Westerville, Ohio: Integrity Press, 1991–96.

Ringling Brothers and Barnum and Bailey Combined Circus. *Route Book for the Season of 1939*. [Sarasota, Fla.: Joseph Mayer, Publisher, [1939].

———. *Route, Personnel, and Statistics for the Season of 1964*. New York: Ringling Brothers and Barnum and Bailey Press Department, 1964.

Russell, Ross. *Jazz Style in Kansas City and the Southwest*. Berkley: University of California Press, 1971.

Rust, Brian. *Jazz Records, 1897–1942*. 4th rev. and enl. ed. Vol. 2. New Rochelle, N.Y.: Arlington House, 1978.

Seroff, Doug. "Gospel Arts Day Nashville: A Special Commemoration" [program]. Fisk University, Nashville, Tenn., June 19, 1988.

Short, Ernest Henry. *Fifty Years of Vaudeville*. Westport, Conn.: Greenwood, 1978.

Sobel, Bernard. *A Pictorial History of Vaudeville*. New York: Citadel, 1961.

Southern, Eileen. *Biographical Dictionary of Afro-American and African Musicians*. Westport, Conn.: Greenwood, 1982.

———. *The Music of Black Americans: A History*. New York: Norton, 1971.

Stearns, Marshall W. *The Story of Jazz*. New York: Oxford University Press, 1956.

Titon, Jeff Todd, ed. *Worlds of Music: An Introduction to the Music of the World's Peoples*. New York: Schirmer, 1984.

Trotter, Joe William, Jr., ed. *The Great Migration in Historical Perspective: New Dimensions of Race, Class, and Gender*. Bloomington: Indiana University Press, 1991.

Watkins, Clifford Edward, I. *Circus Benediction*. Greensboro, NC: EdCliff Publications, 1995.

———. "Marching Bands." Cited in *Encyclopedia of African-American Culture and History*, ed. Jack Salzman, David Lionel Smith, and Cornel West. New York: Macmillan, 1995.

———. *The Works of Three Selected Band Directors in Predominantly Black American Colleges and Universities*. Ann Arbor, Mich.: University Microfilms International, 1975.

———. "P. G. Lowery and His Musical Enterprises: The Formative Years." Cited in *Feel the Spirit: Studies in Nineteenth Century Afro-American Music*, ed. George Keck and Sherrill V. Martin. New York: Greenwood, 1988.

Whiteman, Barbara A. "A Treasury of Black Dolls from Yesterday to Today" [exhibit notes]. Philadelphia Doll Museum, Philadelphia Free Library, 1992.

Wintz, William D. *Nitro, the World War I Boom Town: An Illustrated History of Nitro, West Virginia, and the Land on Which It Stands*. Charleston, W. Va.: Pictorial Histories, 1985.

Woll, Allen. *Black Musical Theatre: From Coontown to Dreamgirls*. Baton Rouge: Louisiana State University Press, 1989.

Wood, Charles L. *The Kansas Beef Industry*. Lawrence: Regents Press of Kansas, 1980.

Zimmerman, Jack. "Notes from Northfield." *Instrumentalist* (February 1991).

INTERVIEWS

Hooks, Benjamin. Telephone interview by author, Memphis, Tenn., March 1995.

Parkinson, Tom. Telephone interview by author. Tape recording, Savoy, Ill., December 31, 1992.

Seymour, William. Interview by author, Boston, Mass., November 21, 1994.

INDEX